Around our Southern Table
A Southern Escoffier

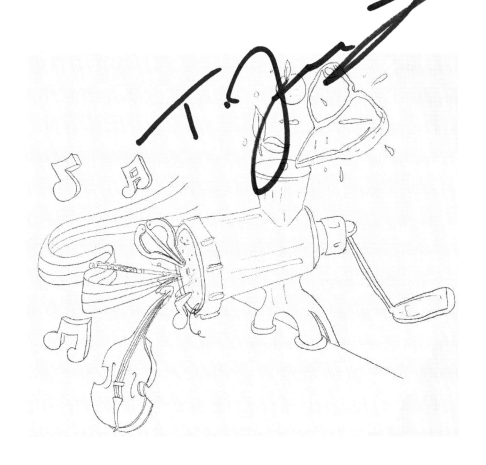

T. Jensen Lacey
(with Eric Lacey)

T. Jensen Lacey

WWW.MOONHOWLERPUBLISHING.COM
PO BOX 1175, FAIRHOPE, AL 36533

ISBN: 978-1-7342111-6-0

FV-7

"Front and back cover art by J. D. Crowe.
Interior line drawings by Charles Hudson Davis.

Manufactured in the United States

COOKBOOK TABLE OF CONTENTS

T. Jensen Lacey

INTRODUCTION

From Theresa (T. Jensen Lacey)

I first began writing this cookbook in 1982, scrawling stories and recipes in a University of Alabama Super Store notebook left over from one of my classes I was taking back then. In those years, groceries cost me and my roommate about $70 a week for both of us, gas was about fifty-three cents a gallon and I bought a used car with a hole in the radiator for $100 (I had to refill the radiator to get back home from classes). Back then, I was just making notes of recipes, which were really observations from watching my grandmother and great-aunts and -uncles cook in the kitchen or on the grill. None of them had anything resembling a cookbook, had never had one, and scoffed at anyone suggesting they either go by or write down a recipe.

My friend Rick Bragg was the one who gave me the push to get this cookbook finalized. Over the years, I had been to virtually every one of his readings and signings, and once he even invited me to sit with him up on the stage (The Venue, Fairhope, 2019). It was this night he read from his newly-released book, *The Best Cook in the World: Tales from My Momma's Table* (2018, Knopf). Hearing his words from the Introduction, I was suddenly transported to his momma's kitchen:

> *She cooked for dead-broke uncles, hungover brothers, shadetree mechanics, faith healers, dice shooters, hairdressers, pipe fitters, crop dusters, high-steel walkers, and well diggers.*

and later, on the next page, the words that hit me, as they say, "where I lived":

> *She cooked with ghosts at her sure right hand.*

That was when I knew I needed to get on paper and in a book some of my people's recipes, and a few memories to go with them if I could remember them. As I wrote at the keyboard, my own people's ghosts beside me, I knew I was writing something that would be important to the people I'd be leaving behind, maybe some people not even born yet and whom I would never meet, but they'd read these pages and maybe try a recipe or two, and make the circle complete.

It was in the fall of 2021 that Rick was in town again (but keeping his distance due to COVID), doing a reading of his book *Speckled Beauty*, a dog that he said he hated but in truth it turned out to be a love story of a sort. When he was leaving Page & Palette (the bookstore), out on the sidewalk I hailed him and thanked him for inspiring me to finish this cookbook, which now covers several generations. He just smiled, said "I'm glad to know that," and got in his car to leave town.

I

Around our Southern Table
A Southern Escoffier

CHAPTER 1

PROCESS, INGREDIENTS, PREPARATION & PRESENTATION

by Eric Lacey

Every recipe is just basically a process – a process of preparing food to achieve a particular end result. Therefore, a philosophy of process has to be adopted that will provide the framework for a successful outcome. One of the hallmarks of our family is that we sit down at the dinner table every night (unless we go out – which is rare). It's the gathering of people to share a meal – and it's the time a family shares their souls – to enlighten others with a story, or reminisce of times and people gone before.

Even now with an empty nest, Theresa and I share a meal – almost every evening. We ask for blessings and guidance first, then it's time to enjoy. It's from necessity that many of these recipes were developed. No one wants to gather around a table to share a crappy meal. That doesn't happen in our house. It is the glue that brought us together and keeps us in touch.

It seems perhaps rudimentary to start with something so basic, but in these times of instant gratification and "click here" answers, much has been lost which won't be passed down – unless someone states the obvious. And, being sometimes referred to as "Captain Obvious," I would be remiss if I didn't start at the beginning.

These recipes are all prepared and edited with the following in mind:

1) The reader reviews the ingredients, reads the recipe and decides what tweaks may be necessary, due to time or ingredient constraints.

2) All ingredients are gathered and prepared – as much as possible – in advance. All the slicing and dicing, finding ingredients, and making sure there is enough, running to the store again, dividing into applications, melting the butter, preparing the stock - everything that can be done before the actual combination of ingredients and preparing of the recipe – is done. We won't lecture too much on this – but it makes cooking so much more enjoyable when you have what you need. There are "happy accidents" and the course of human history – much less gastronomy has been changed due to adaptations, so in the end, it's "what you got" – right?

3) Except where indicated, quantities are subject to taste and dietary preferences. We like things on the savory side of the scale, so we seldom add sugar or sweetener – and then only in small incremental amounts. Additionally, we find there is way too much salt in many preparations--and in some ingredients, so we seldom add salt to a recipe. It can

always be added "to taste" afterward. On the discussion of salt, we use unsalted butter – exclusively. In dishes with cheese especially, any additional salt will result in a final dish that tastes like brine. We apply Chachere's to a lot of preparations – which has as its base, salt. Therefore we use only a tiny amount – because it is very finely ground and also gives its chili pepper kick – which acts like salt on the taste buds.

4) In choosing your flour (All Purpose or AP, or Self-Rising or SR in the recipes), we strongly suggest you buy unbromated and unbleached flours. Bromine, an ingredient which helps prevent caking in flour, is also a potent carcinogen (cancer-causing agent), as is bleach. Who wants to feed their friends and family that?

INGREDIENTS

1) *Wine*: if you won't drink it, don't use it. In fact, I usually add wine from my own glass. The exception would be – perhaps a marsala, which is usually too salty to enjoy straight. The concept of "leftover" wine may have some value, but it's one we haven't been able to assess.

2) *Vinegar* is a wonderful ingredient, and it is useful to keep an array of vinegars on hand. I tend to use the unflavored varieties – so I can control the final flavor and not count on a vinegar base to deliver it. Raspberry vinegar is fine if you are making a raspberry vinaigrette dressing (which I don't like anyway), but otherwise... My stock includes vinegars as follows:

> Apple Cider (not pulpy)
> Aceto Balsamico (Balsamic Italian)
> Rice wine
> Red Wine Vinegar
> Champagne vinegar

3) *Oils* are also a basic ingredient in many recipes. Again, fusions are useful, but I find it easier to control taste and texture by not counting on an oil to provide a featured flavor. For example, I have been given several small bottles of lemon infused olive oil. I just can't bring myself to use them. If I want to use some olive oil, then I use it – and if I want a lemon flavor, I use fresh lemon juice, zest, or lemon juice from the fridge. The one exception is truffle oil. So, in my stock there are 6 kinds of oil:
Wesson pure vegetable oil (sauté frying, salad dressings – where the oil isn't the flavor)

> Extra Virgin Olive Oil (small amounts, always)
> EVOO infused truffle oil (get the smallest amount you can- it doesn't keep long)
> Bacon grease (yes, save that fat when you fry bacon – I use it a lot)
> Peanut oil (or Canola) for those high temp applications – i.e. deep-frying fish
> Sesame oil

4) *Sauces* are also highly necessary and usually end up adding a salty, umami (savory) base to some of these recipes. I could write a chapter on hot sauces alone – but my 2 "go to" are readily available in most stores and give the 2 spectrums of spice with vinegar sour kick (Crystal) and vinegar spice with real kick (Tabasco). One quick mention – most of these sauces are potent – and can ruin a dish in a dash. When adding, use a small spoon, add a little at a time – usually toward the end of a recipe. Like salt, put the sauce on the table and let connoisseurs add their own.

My stock includes

Soy Sauce (Low sodium doesn't make any difference – get the good stuff and add sparingly)
Fish Sauce (again, get the good stuff)
Thai Chili Garlic – Srirachi is what I use
Worcestershire – Got to have it on hand
Crystal
Tabasco

5) *Butter*: as mentioned, always unsalted, in stick form, if we are below 2 sticks in the fridge, we are in the "red zone."

6) *Dairy* is a whole 'nother category – we keep a lot of dairy on hand for numerous things we consume daily. What we have in the fridge and ready most of the time:

Half and half
Heavy whipping cream
Whole pasteurized buttermilk (ignore the expiration date – before you shake it, open the cap and look inside. If the buttermilk doesn't have a "blue cap" (mold) on the top of the milk, shake well and rock on. A quart can last for months.
Cheese in shredded form, extra sharp/sharp cheddar, "taco/Mexican," "Italian," Parmesan, and mozzarella.
Cheese in solid form, Feta, good blue cheese (Maytag if available), Chevre, Cream Cheese.
For breads, especially yeast bread, we will use a blend of *powdered* Parmesan and Romano cheeses

7) *Condiments* are sometimes ingredients, and it can be a real disaster if assumptions are made about taste – without tasting or considering the consequences.
Mayonnaise – we have found the cheaper store brands are the best. "Piggly Wiggly," Bama, Dukes, etc. These are usually produced regionally. Never- ever – use Miracle Whip.

Mustard – we keep store brand, yellow mustard and Dijon on hand. You can spend all you want on this stuff, but the results are the same….

Ketchup – we read the labels – not a fan of high fructose corn syrup and try hard to avoid it in stuff we buy – hard to avoid in ketchup – and I really don't like sweet ketchup. I really like "Whataburger" brand spicy ketchup, but it's a little hard to find and definitely more expensive than the main brands. It isn't really spicy – just not sweet…

Pickles – Must have dill relish as well as dill pickles on hand – we stock "Wickles" brand relish and burger chips as well as Claussen sandwich slices on hand – for all occasions be prepared!

Olives – Kalamata, pitted, as well as Green Spanish olives – pitted. I wonder why unpitted olives are even sold.

Pimientos

PREPARATION

Knives: A sharp knife is a blessing; a dull one, a curse. Big knives make fast work. Small knives produce small results. Both are very appropriate to their tasks. We use very good steel, kept very sharp. Never put your good steel knives in a dishwasher, sink, or utensil drawer. When done with a knife, wash immediately and replace in a butcher block or other safe storage. If dulled, touch with steel before storing. Never cut onto stone surfaces. Wood or plastic (starboard is great) for veggies; use hard plastic only for meats (reason being, hard plastic can be sterilized of any bacteria the meat might have).

Other essential tools: a good peeler (I have a treasured "CUTCO") is a necessity. A collection of footed steel colanders, a couple of mesh strainers, plastic spatula for use with non-stick, slotted spoons, etc. Over time you will accumulate more than you need and find what you use is the same 6-10 pieces, over and over.

Cross contamination from meats can be deadly. While cooking can be a generous act of love, if care is not taken, it can poison yourself and those who consume your art. Don't do it! Eggs are in this category. Break a few eggs, wash your hands with soap.

Cutting boards: use only a hard plastic cutting board for meats and decontaminate by washing thoroughly with soap and hot water. Any surface that meat juices touch ***must*** be sterilized before anything else comes in contact. If you use a platter or cookie sheet to prepare some steaks for the grill, after you put the steaks on the grill, wash the platter (and your hands). It doesn't matter if it is beef, chicken, fish – or any other critter – keep it clean.

Some easy ways to deal with ingredients to avoid problems of cross contamination we use every day:

Meat preparation on a cookie sheet or platter – cover it with aluminum foil first. When the meat is transferred to the grill or cooking vessel, remove and discard the foil and you now have a clean vessel to work with.

When chopping veggies and "prepping," we use waxed paper plates. In a recipe where there are chopped onions, and cabbage, as well as minced garlic, chopped olives and diced herbs, the big stuff can be kept on one plate and the little stuff on another – ready to add when the time comes – and the plates (if dry) can be used as covers for stuff put in the microwave to reheat – or to cover finished items to help retain heat. When done, toss. Remember – paper is from trees – the ONLY material we have that is renewable, regenerative, and recyclable.

When preparing food, especially baked goods, there is often a tendency to forget what's in the oven or under the broiler. This can result in a burned dish, wasted food, disappointed diners and a smelly house (as anyone knows who's tried to get the burnt odor from their homes and kitchens). Here's a hack offered by our daughter, Sarah Lacey Jones, to avoid burning virtually anything.

When you put something in the oven, especially if it's on "broil," put an oven mitt on one of your hands–and keep it on there until you have removed the dish from the oven. This simple technique will remind you that there's something in the oven and you will never burn anything! This trick has saved many a dish from burning.

PRESENTATION

Finally, we have become converts to the "heated plate and serving dish" for dishes served hot. Yes, it is a little more hassle to deal with hot plates, but the results are easy to justify. A sizzling steak put on a cold plate – ceases to sizzle. A piping hot lasagna loses its lava goodness, and all that time taken to prepare it is partially lost. I've found that eating fast is a symptom of food losing its proper temperature. If it is served hot, on a heated plate, more time can be taken to enjoy it – and the company you keep. Likewise, a nicely prepared wedge salad on a chilled salad plate deserves its place in the serving discussion.

Plates are nice when matching and everything is color coordinated. Setting a fine table is an art in itself, but not what this book is about. When the occasion is appropriate, we will spend some time on the table and the results are always appreciated. However, it is always about the food, and if the effort is put forth, genuinely and with love, the result will always speak for itself. It takes time – the one currency we cannot replace, and in the giving of it, may it bring joy to those who receive the fruits of your effort.

Most of these recipes serve 4-6 adults. They state otherwise if you're serving two people or ten.

We decided against offering nutritional information per serving size. We eat to enjoy a well-made dish, and everything we've made tends to be more on the healthy side, anyway. We've found that we cook dishes when a particular vegetable is in season (just ask anyone from Lower Alabama when Silver Queen Corn is here, and they can tell you to the last day), and fresh food is always better-tasting and more nutritious than frozen or, Lord forbid, canned (unless home-canned).

CHAPTER 2

GADGETS, GIZMOS AND GOT-TO-HAVES
(COOKING APPURTENANCES/APPERATI)

Since we are trying to pass along some well-earned experiences with food, we need to discuss some methods of actual cooking that are real "game changers." It wouldn't be fair to just jump into a cookbook and not discuss some of the best ways to do the actual cooking.

PRESSURE COOKER/INSTANT POT:

Gone are the days of fear and trepidation when grandma used to pull out the huge pressure cooker - or canner as it was sometimes called. That big pot with the pressure valve on top, which was always deployed with stern warnings for the kids to stay out of the kitchen, in case the damn thing exploded. We now have "instant cookers" with electronic controls that dial in the right temperature, time and pressure for consistent and safe results. We love ours - it isn't an air fryer - we aren't THAT modern - but find it irreplaceable for cooking pork butts, ribs, and other fantastic proteins in a reasonable time frame. There's a Carnitas recipe in the chapter on "MEATS AND STEWS" that utilizes the pressure cooker. If you have one, there are many other uses as well.

SOUS VIDE COOKER:

If you have ever been to a really high-end steak house with several people and they each order their different cuts cooked to differing levels of doneness, the miracle is in the method of cooking: sous vide. The principle is that the meat is brought to a uniform temperature - across the entire piece of meat - then finished to a level of doneness on a flat top or charcoal grill. It's a real game changer - steaks and fish that are perfectly done, through and through, all at the same approximate time, ready to eat.

This can only be achieved by heating - without air or French for "under vacuum" (Sous Vide). The meat is not dried out as its juices migrate out and evaporate. The meat is also not overheated above the level of doneness desired. It's not a very expensive gadget - about the same as an instant pot. One of my best Christmas gifts from daughter Sarah and son Gus.

MEAT THERMOMETER:

I know it seems rudimentary, but there are still legions of brothers out there who cook dishes based on how they "look." That's backwards, unnecessary, and for $20 you too can be a master of the smoked chicken, grilled pork chop or baked pork tenderloin. Get a digital meat thermometer that has a probe and 3-4' of wire lead to it. When your baked chicken has been in the oven for 30 or so minutes, put that probe into the breast down by the thigh an inch or so deep. Set the monitor beside the stove and set the temp alarm to 155 degrees and forget it until it goes off. Then, watch the monitor till it gets to 165 and remove it from the oven - a perfectly done bird! The difference is amazing - cooking until internal temperature is reached - instead of how it looks! Trust me - this is the easiest and cheapest "hack" there is. Another plus is, since you're not cooking based on appearance of the meat, and instead on the actual temperature, you're more certain to get a dish done to a perfect turn without any dryness. Guests around our table constantly mention this ("How'd you get this done without it being dry?" they'll ask.).

RICE COOKER:

Thirty plus years ago I came home from work with a bag of groceries from MiMi's Asian Grocery in Clarksville, TN, which wasn't that unusual; however, under my other arm was a box with a Japanese rice cooker in it. Mimi had written the price on the side: $95.00. Theresa was rather incensed that I had spent so much (in 1990 dollars) on a rice cooker. Within a few years she settled down about it. We still use it probably 2 times a week. Makes rice perfectly every time. She isn't mad any longer about its purchase.

WOK:

For Christmas many years ago, Theresa bought me a very nice non-stick wok with a lid. I use it probably 2X a month. When you need a wok, a frying pan is a poor substitute.

CAST IRON:

It's heavy, has been in and out of style so many times - it still isn't equaled in cooking preparations - cast iron for us is legacy cookware. I have a 12" skillet that was my grandmother's until she couldn't pick it up any longer. I have a 24" skillet that I have to use 2 hands for. Our Dutch Oven is one of our most treasured possessions. We even have cast iron corn-pone pans. Cardinal rule: do not wash with soap! Hot water only! If something is hopelessly stuck, pour some boiling water into the cast ironware, scrape well and re-season with cooking oil and put in a warm oven (this opens the "pores" of the cast iron and allows the oil to penetrate for a good seal).

With regular use and minimal care, your cast ironware will outlast you. And as long as my kids are around, our cast iron collection will serve yet another generation. Note to readers: buy the best cast iron (such as Lodge), or get one at an estate sale or, like us, from a relative who no longer cooks.

GREEN EGG - OR GRILL WITH SMOKING POSSIBILITIES

About 15 years ago my brother, sister and father gave me a Green Egg for my birthday. They were clever! Not only has it been a staple in my cooking repertoire, they have enjoyed many meals from it as well. They are expensive, but I can attest, they really hold up for a long time. I've only replaced the felt gasket once (needs it again) and will soon need to replace the lid ring, but that is after hundreds of uses and rarely any attention. I don't have all the fancy gadgets that can go with the grill - I just put a coffee can of water in the center of the fire ring if I want to smoke something, and choke the air flow down. Works great. For grilling steak or chicken, roasting veggies or fish, the only additional item I use regularly is a grill pan - one of those pans with holes in it - so that my asparagus or sliced peppers don't fall through to the fire. I spray it with non-stick first and it mostly doesn't get sticky.

CHAPTER 3:

THE HERB GARDEN

Depending on the climate and setting of your abode, if possible, a small herb garden can add a major kick to everything you cook. Every evening when prepping for dinner, I take some scissors and harvest what I will use. It's a very satisfying act in itself. And a big handful of fresh cut herbs is something to share when you bring it inside. What you cultivate is highly dependent on your growing season and position (sunlight availability, mainly), and all we can highlight is what grows well in LA (Lower Alabama).

Our house/lot is situated amongst huge live oaks and longleaf pines. Most of the yard is shaded except on the south side - which is the front of the house. I've taken some old treated wooden gates to use as a platform in the sea of ivy that grows in the yard, placing an old wash pot for the Italian and Thai Basil on one edge,

and multiple 8" and 10" clay pipes, stood on end and filled with good topsoil around the other edges. That's my herb garden. The Rosemary is now a bush - and anchors one corner of the front garden. The oregano is filling in below our bushes immediately in front of the house - as ground cover and awesome spice. Another oregano, left to its own devices and mostly neglected, has grown out of the confines of its pot and is thriving and creeping happily along the walkway by the front door. Lavender, for us, seems to be the "pickiest" of the herbs. Although we planted it in a sunny, well-drained spot at the southern edge of the garden, it's often the one to complain the most (about it being too dry, too hot, ad infinitum), by not growing as well as the other herbs. The best I can do for this one is to cut it back in late summer every year. Pruning does seem to help most herbs.

Speaking of pruning, it's important to keep in mind that herbs that flower, such as basil, need to be trimmed before they flower, because it's then that they "bolt" and will go to seed. You want to use your productive herbs as long as possible, thus, trim them when you see the first buds appear–unless, of course, you want blossoms from them, such as the aforementioned lavender.

SPRING/SUMMER/FALL

Combining these seasons because they are the main growing season here in the deep south. March/April are safe for setting out started plants. We buy them from our local herb grower. They need regular water - at least 1 time every 2 days in the hot season. I fertilize with Miracle Grow every 3-4 weeks. Here's what we plant and why:

Oregano: Super versatile, easy to grow, thrives on neglect and will stay alive year 'round.
Thyme: like Oregano, hearty and so useful
Lemon Grass: Beautiful, long leaves, if it doesn't get nipped by frost, will live year 'round
Mint: Great in so many things - again, with proper cutting back it will live year 'round
Rosemary: We have a bush that is 16 years old. Not the prettiest thing, but resilient and very useful
Sage: in mixed sunlight - growing beside my lemongrass this has done well year 'round
Italian Basil: plant 3-4 plants together in a big pot in March/April- I tend to over harvest - it won't last much past October. Keep the seed heads pinched off.
Thai Basil: Plant 3-4 plants in March/April. Keep the purple flowers/seed heads pinched off. Will die off in November
Chili peppers/Jalapeno peppers: Again, plant 3-4 plants in a larger pot and they will thrive through the season. We have Jalapenos still growing at Christmas.

October: The time to pull out what's dying off and put in some things that will thrive.

Dill: always buy 2-3 plants and combine in a medium pot. It will do great.
Chervil: great French herb
Parsley: great to have
Chives: so useful in so many dishes

Options that are available, but we don't plant:

Anais (can't stand any licorice flavor)
Tarragon: same
Tomatoes: It pains me to admit, but I can't grow tomatoes better than those I can buy. They take up so much space and time - and bear fruit for so short a time - support your local farmer's market and buy their tomatoes.
Cilantro: When I need it - I need a lot, so I either overharvest, or it goes to seed too quickly.

Besides the rosemary, which is a bush, and the oregano, which is doing its own thing under our front bushes, this herb garden only takes up a 4' X 8' square. It sits right in front of our main entryway, so I see it constantly and know when it needs watering, or the basil heads need pinching. Many meals are decided based on herbs that need to be cut back/harvested.

Coming back from the farmer's market with some fine summer tomatoes, seeing the basil full and healthy and inspiration hits: Tomatoes Caprese, or tomatoes, basil and feta salad, or - you get the idea…

Even the most accomplished cooks will find that adding an herb garden to their dwelling, even if it is a window-box, will enhance their cooking experience and delight their guests' taste buds.

CHAPTER 4

APPETIZERS & BEVERAGES

CHEESE STRAWS
This is one of Jeanne Franklin Lacey's (Eric's Mom's) recipes.

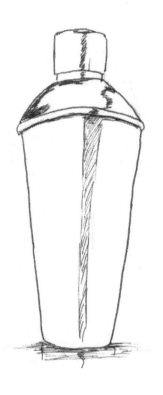

    1 C sifted all-purpose flour
    ½ t baking powder
    ½ C butter
    1 C shredded cheddar cheese
    ¼ t cayenne pepper (optional)
    3 T cold water

Sift flour and baking powder into a bowl; cut in butter and cheese like you would do for a pie crust, using a pastry blender or two knives. Add water and mix well. Fill cookie press. Form straws on parchment paper using a star plate. Cut into desired lengths. Bake. Remove to cooling racks and cool completely before storing.

CINDY BARNETT LACEY'S CHEESE CRISPS
Eric's brother Richard's wife Cindy says this is one of her favorite recipes, and it's always a hit at parties or tailgates.

    1 ½ sticks butter, unsalted, at room temperature so it's soft
    1 lb sharp cheddar cheese, finely grated
    2 C AP flour
    1 t cayenne pepper
    ½ t salt
    2 C toasted (crispy) rice cereal (such as Rice Krispies)

Preheat oven to 350 degrees. Move the two oven racks to the middle and lower third of the oven. In a mixing bowl, beat the softened butter and cheddar cheese at low to medium speed until well-combined. Add flour, pepper and salt; beat until the mixture resembles crumbly dough. Add the rice cereal and mix thoroughly.

Make balls out of the dough, using a large tablespoon and put on greased cookie sheets. Press dough so they make round shapes roughly two inches in diameter.

Bake crisps for about 25 minutes, changing cookie sheets about halfway through (top to bottom and vice versa) so neither over- or under-bakes. When golden brown, remove from oven and cool completely on cookie sheets. When cooled, remove from cookie sheets and store in airtight containers (such as Zip-Loc). Enjoy within a week.

TOP-OF-THE-MORNING ORANGE SMOOTHIE
(From Theresa)
I made this nearly every morning of my early college years. It's a perfect and quick meal replacement, and is low-fat, high-fiber and refreshing, too!

1 small can frozen orange juice, unsweetened
1 additional can water (about 6-8 ounces)
1 C frozen, plain strawberries
1 C whole buttermilk

Whirl all of the above in a blender until it's the consistency you like. Pour into glasses and enjoy. Makes enough for 2-3 servings. Chill any remaining to enjoy later.

DINNER-ON-THE-GROUNDS DEVILED EGGS
(From Theresa)
Every Memorial Day weekend, my people would gather at our family cemetery in north Alabama. We'd clean and decorate the gravesites and tombstones of those who'd gone before. After we were finished, we'd share a meal, where everybody brought something. This deviled egg recipe has been in my family for generations, but variations, influenced by family members with "other" backgrounds and cultures, are below.

Makes 24:
12 eggs, boiled, cooled, and peeled
1 C mayonnaise
2 T lemon juice
Salt and pepper to taste
¼ C Dill relish
Paprika

Slice the eggs in half; gently scoop out the cooked yolk into a bowl. Place the cooked whites on a deviled egg tray, open side up. Mix the yolks with the mayonnaise, lemon juice, S&P and dill relish. Add more mayonnaise if it's not creamy enough to your liking. Dust with paprika. Keep chilled and covered until ready to serve.

VARIATIONS: Use Tony Chachere's to add a Cajun flavor. Substitute sweet relish for dill, or mix it half and half, for a sweeter flavor. Add 1 can (drained and chopped) water chestnuts for a crunchy, Asian twist, or add ¼ C chopped celery. Add ¼ C finely diced sweet onion. You can add ½ C finely chopped bacon bits. Use Smoked Paprika for a depth of flavor. You may also substitute (plain) Greek yogurt for mayonnaise. Any way you make these, you are guaranteed to come home with an empty serving dish and a smile of satisfaction.

LIBATIONS:

BROTHER RICHARD'S BAHAMA BLOODY
(served on brother Richard and wife Cindy's vessel, WooHoo, and also on Scotland Cay, a private island in the Abacos)

Note: can use just tequila or vodka, or even rum. Noted below as regularly served when provisions are abundant.

  1 shot good vodka
  1 shot good tequila
  3 shots Clamato
  Dash tabasco
  Dash Worcestershire
  Juice of half a squeezed lime
  Dash Adobo seasoning
  Fresh squeezed lime to taste

Serve over ice. Try to sip. One is good, two is great, three is nap time.

SHOMO RUSSIAN
Served at the old camp (Shomo) after returning from the morning hunt, after breakfast and before nap.

1:1:1 ratio vodka, Kahlua and half/half, add ice, shake well.

ECHO LANE MARGARITA

1 ½ shot tequila (don't spend a lot!)
Juice of 2 limes
1 t sugar (can be skipped if you don't mind heavy lime)

Combine and stir thoroughly. Pour into medium insulated glass over ice. Top with soda water.

QND (quick and dirty) OLD FASHIONED

2 shots of good bourbon
3 dashes of orange bitters
A bit of lemon juice to taste

Serve over ice. Top off with soda water.

CHAPTER 5

BREADS

MOTHER THERESA'S CHEESY 6-ITALIAN-HERB BREAD

I perfected this recipe during Thanksgiving of 2010. It is made with distilled water, organic, NON-BROMATED and UNBLEACHED bread flour, pure cane sugar, sea salt, and grated (powdered) Parmesan and Romano cheeses. The herbs are basil, marjoram, oregano, rosemary, sage and thyme.

There are two versions of this recipe: one for if you want to bake the bread immediately, and another for freezing the dough, to thaw and bake at a later date. Here they both are.

I use a bread machine, not to bake the bread, but to put it through the mixing and first-rising process, as the bread texture is more uniform than if I (impatient self that I am) mix it by hand. Set your bread machine to "Dough," and, IN THIS ORDER, put the following in the pan:

> 1 C warm water (should not be so hot that it burns your fingers)
> 2 ¾ C unbromated, unbleached bread flour (King Arthur or White Lily is good)
> 1 T sugar
> 1 ½ t salt
> ¼ C total grated Romano and Parmesan cheeses (in powdered form)

2 T EACH oregano, basil, marjoram, thyme, rosemary and sage
2 T unsalted butter, cut into halves (so you have four halves)
1 heaping T yeast (I use Red Star)

After all this is in your pan, put the pan in the machine, turning to set in place. Press "Start" and "Lock" and close lid. My machine has the dough ready in 1 ½ hours.

After dough is ready and has gone through its first rising, take it out of the pan. If dough is still sticky, add a dusting of bread flour to it. Knead a minute or two on a cutting board dusted with flour. Shape into loaf and, with seam side down, place loaf into a greased loaf pan (turning once to get some of the grease on the top of the dough).

Place in a warm oven and allow to rise a second time. DO NOT OPEN OVEN DOOR! After it's risen a second time (roughly 35-45 minutes), set the oven to 350. Bake for 30 minutes or until loaf is golden brown on the outside and sounds hollow when tapped on top. Pop out of the loaf pan onto a cooling rack. Serve whenever you like (my family LOVES bread fresh and hot out of the oven).

This next section is for dough that you let go through the mixing-and-rising stage, and that you froze to bake later (I freeze my dough in half-gallon Zip-Loc bags, sprayed on the inside with olive-oil flavored non-stick).

This dough has already been through one rising. **Instructions for finishing the loaf:**

The night before you want to bake this bread, take loaf out of freezer. Place loaf (still in Zip-Loc bag) in refrigerator and let thaw there 6 hours, or overnight.

About two hours before serving, take loaf out of Zip-Loc bag; lightly knead (only about a minute) on a cutting board dusted with flour. Form into loaf, put in greased loaf pan, place in WARM (not hot) oven and allow to rise for the second and final time. This usually takes about 35 minutes but allow 1-1/2 hours, since you've started from a frozen loaf.

When loaf is doubled in size, set oven to 350 degrees. Bake, uncovered, for about 35-45 minutes or until loaf is golden brown and sounds hollow when tapped on top.

NOTE: Once you've put loaf in warm oven to rise, DO NOT open oven; this will let a draft in and the loaf will fall (it will still bake okay, but will be denser and not as fluffy). Also, this dough makes a fantastic dough for homemade PIZZA.

HOMEMADE CROUTONS
We made these using some of my leftover bread, the recipe for which is above.

4 slices homemade or other artisan bread, thinly sliced (to about ¼" thickness)
4 T butter
Dash garlic powder

½ C each mozzarella and parmesan cheeses, thinly sliced

Spread equal amounts of butter on each slice of bread; place slices on baking pan lined with parchment paper (you will have a sticky mess if you use foil). Sprinkle slices with garlic powder; cover each slice with mozzarella slices. Turn broiler on "low" and broil until mozzarella is melted but not burned. Pull out pan and add parmesan cheese; put in broiler, this time set on "high," and keep a close eye as it can burn quickly. Remove from oven when the cheese is browned to your liking.

Put slices on cutting board; cut into pieces as a topping for salads or on top of a good, hearty soup (we used these on top of our French Onion Soup, in Chapter 12).

MOM'S BUTTERMILK BISCUITS
(Theresa's mom)
My mom shared this with me in June 2021.

> 4 cups AP flour
> 5 t. baking powder
> 1 t. salt
> ¾ t. baking soda
> 3 T. Crisco, melted & cooled
> 2 C buttermilk (whole)

Sift together first 4 ingredients; add Crisco and stir in buttermilk to form into a ball. Flour a large cutting board (or a clean countertop) and place dough in center. Knead lightly just until no longer sticky (if you knead dough too much, the biscuits will come out tough and chewy). Roll out dough into half-inch thickness; cut with biscuit-cutter (I use a clean tuna can). Place biscuits, sides touching* into sprayed pan. Dot tops of biscuits with butter. Place pan in preheated oven and bake at 425 degrees for 12-15 minutes, until biscuits are golden brown.

*If you place the biscuits apart from each other, they will spread OUT rather than UP, resulting in a dry, dense biscuit. When they rise UP, they will be fluffy and tender!

ZUCCHINI BREAD
Another one of my mom's recipes that she shared with me June 2021.

> 3 large eggs
> 2 C sugar or monk-fruit sweetener
> 1 C oil
> 2 t. vanilla
> 2 C zucchini, washed, peeled and grated or shredded
> 8 oz. can pineapple, crushed, drained
> 3 C AP flour
> 2 t. baking soda
> 1 t. salt

½ t. baking powder
2 t. cinnamon
1 C walnuts or pecans, chopped

In a large bowl, combine all dry ingredients and set aside. In another large bowl, beat eggs; add sugar, oil and vanilla and beat until creamy, then add dry ingredients and blend well. Add nuts; stir in pineapple and zucchini. Pour into two well-greased and floured 9x5x3" baking pans. Bake at 350 degrees for one hour or until light brown on top and they pass the "toothpick test." Remove from oven, let rest for 10 minutes, then remove loaves from pans and cool on a bread rack.

Mom says this bread freezes well—if there's any left!

ERIC'S CORNBREAD OR CORN PONES--WITH VARIATIONS

No Southern cook would consider themselves well-versed in classic Southern dishes if they couldn't turn out a decent type of cornbread. Many old-timers in the South would have leftover, cold cornbread as a type of cereal, sprinkled with a little sugar and doused with milk.

1 ½ C real cornmeal (we use Claude's Cornmeal, a Fairhope staple available at Old Tyme Feed and Seed)
½ C all-purpose flour
1 T baking powder
1 t salt
2 eggs beaten
1 ½ C buttermilk
½ C milk (or 2 C buttermilk is better....)
¼ C vegetable oil

For the skillet:
1 T bacon fat

Combine all dry ingredients in a large mixing bowl; blend well with a fork

Separately combine all wet ingredients, blend well with a fork, then combine with dry ingredients, blending with a spoon to make sure there are no dry ingredient pockets. Adjust with more buttermilk if batter is too thick - we like our cornbread moist, not dry, so it can take up to ¼ cup more - keep stirring until desired consistency is reached.

Let stand 30 minutes or so.

Meanwhile, preheat oven to 400 degrees, place bacon fat in a seasoned 12" cast iron skillet and put in oven. Heat until it just begins to smoke. Swirl grease around in skillet to coat.

Remove skillet and pour cornbread batter in right away - you should hear the batter sizzle as you are creating an outer crust on the cornbread. Place in oven and bake 20-30 minutes. It is done when the top is brown and it passes the toothpick test. Remove and let stand at least 10 minutes before cutting into pie slices.

Notes:

Pones: this makes about a dozen pones. Just make sure you put plenty of bacon grease in each pone and only fill ½ way with batter.

Muffins: Makes about 12 muffins - put some bacon fat in every muffin hole - again, only fill ½ way with cornbread batter.

"Mexican" cornbread:
Combine wet ingredients as noted above, but add:

> 1 C drained canned corn (can be white or yellow)
> 1 small jar chopped pimientos, drained
> 1 small can chopped green chiles, drained
> 2 jalapenos, chopped
> ½ C Vidalia onion chopped
> ¼ bell pepper, chopped
> 1 cup shredded "taco" style cheese

Sweat the onion, bell pepper and jalapeno. When cooled, blend well with wet ingredients, add to dry ingredients, add buttermilk as needed to achieve desired consistency.

Note: doesn't work well as pones - or muffins - tends to fall apart. It is definitely more "crumbly." No one seems to mind and it is definitely easier to serve from a skillet.

Other notes on cornbread:

Keeps well - after cooling, we cover with aluminum foil and keep in a cool oven overnight. We slice it and reheat it with butter in the oven.

Makes incredible cornbread stuffing.

CORNBREAD STUFFING
This is for a pan of cornbread stuffing - AKA "outside" stuffing, however it could be used to stuff a turkey, duck, a bunch of quail or even Cornish game hens.

> 1 pan cornbread using the above recipe for "Eric's Cornbread" above.
> 1 C chicken stock
> 1 C chicken livers
> 1 C chopped Vidalia onion
> 1 C chopped green bell pepper
> 2 T fresh chopped oregano

3 sprigs fresh sage, chopped
several shakes of black pepper to taste

Boil the chicken livers in the chicken stock until livers are cooked. Dice livers and replace in stock. Sweat the onion and bell peppers, add to the chicken stock

Spray a Pyrex casserole dish with non-stick; add crumbled cornbread, stock and herbs, stir together.

Bake at 400 degrees for 15-20 minutes until heated thoroughly.

If a browned crust is desired, turn on broiler for 5-10 minutes before removing from oven.

Let sit 10 minutes before serving.

SPOON BREAD
This recipe is deceptively simple as well as quick and easy to make. A family member shared this recipe with us decades ago. You can use self-rising cornmeal, omitting the baking powder if you do.

2 C whole milk
1 ½ C water
1 ½ C cornmeal
2 T butter
1 T sugar
1 ½ t salt
5 eggs
1 T baking powder

Spray a 10" cast-iron skillet with nonstick cooking spray and preheat your oven to 350 degrees. In a medium saucepan over low heat, combine water and milk. Stir occasionally until it simmers. Add cornmeal, butter, sugar and salt stir a couple of minutes until thickened; remove from heat.

In a mixing bowl, beat together eggs and baking powder until well combined and fluffy. Stir in cornmeal mixture, mixing well, then spoon into skillet. Bake about 50 minutes but begin checking after about 40 minutes. Bread is done when golden brown on top and it passes the toothpick test. This recipe should serve about 6 people.

Note: If you want your spoonbread crispy on the outside, put 2 T melted butter in your cast iron skillet and leave it in the oven until you're ready to bake the spoonbread. When you "spoon up" the batter into the skillet, it should make a nice sizzling sound. Bake the batter as usual.

CHAPTER 6

CAKES, PIES, COOKIES & DESSERTS

HOMEMADE PIE CRUST
This is Theresa's Mom's recipe. This makes two crusts.

2 ¾ C AP flour
½ t. salt
1/3 C butter-flavored Crisco shortening
1 egg, lightly beaten
7-10 T. ice water

Sift flour and salt together. Add Crisco. With a pastry knife or fingers, blend until pastry is like meal. Mix water with egg. Add cold water/egg mixture one tablespoon at a time until you have a dough that is sticky and holds together (Mom calls this a "firm softball").

Knead on floured surface; divide it in 2 parts. Roll out to desired shape and thickness.

27

NANA'S FRESH APPLE CAKE
(From Theresa)
"Nana"—my Mom—gave me this recipe when she visited us in the summer of 2021.

> 2 C sugar
> 1 ½ C oil
> 2 t. vanilla extract
> 2 eggs, well beaten
> Juice of ½ lemon (or 3 T. from bottled juice)
> 1 t. salt
> 3 C. AP flour
> 1 t. each cinnamon and nutmeg
> 3/4 t. baking soda
> 3 C apples, peeled, cored and diced (about 6 medium)—I used gala
> 1 ½ C pecans, chopped

Combine sugar, oil, vanilla, eggs, lemon juice, and salt. Beat until well blended. Mix flour and soda and add to mixture. Add apples and pecans and mix well. Pour into a tube (bundt) pan which has been greased and dusted with flour. Bake 1 ½ hours at 325 until it passes the toothpick test. Let sit for 10 minutes after removing from oven, then place on wire rack. When cool completely, glaze with the Caramel Glaze, recipe given below.

NANA'S CARAMEL GLAZE
> 1 C sugar or monk fruit sweetener
> ½ c. buttermilk
> ½ t. soda
> 2 T. corn syrup
> ½ C butter, softened
> ½ t. vanilla

Combine all ingredients in a saucepan. Over low heat, bring to a rolling boil, stirring occasionally. Pour over apple cake. Delicious!

APPLESAUCE CAKE MUFFINS
(From Theresa)
My grandmother, Simmie Catherine Parker Bagwell, made this for decades. It was a favorite of my people's, especially my uncles. She never used a recipe, as most folks didn't back then, but she let me watch her as she worked, and I wrote down what she did, so here is the result of those observations.

You can bake this as a regular cake, but muffins are more portable (lunch boxes, etc.), and it seems for those dieting, there's not as much "guilt" as there could be eating a slice of regular cake.

> 2 ½ C AP flour

1 ½ C unsweetened applesauce
1 ¼ C sugar (*if you use sweetened applesauce, omit the sugar*)
½ C stick butter, softened
½ C water
1 ½ t. EACH baking soda and pumpkin pie spice
1 t. salt
¾ t. baking powder
2 large eggs, beaten
1 C golden raisins (optional)
2/3 C chopped nuts

Heat oven to 350. Grease bottom and sides of muffin tins (24 count plus one large muffin tin). Lightly flour. Beat all ingredients except raisins and nuts in large bowl with electric mixer on low speed for 30 seconds, scraping bowl constantly. Beat on high speed for 3 minutes, scraping bowl occasionally. Stir in raisins and nuts. Pour into muffin tins.

Bake muffins for 15 minutes (or in cake pans, 45-50 minutes), or until they pass the toothpick test. Cool. If desired, frost with your favorite frosting, such as a cream-cheese or maple-buttercream (my family likes these muffins just as they are). This produces a very moist product, good served warm with coffee—and the house smells great while the muffins are baking).

SWEET POTATO PIE
This recipe was given to us by our long-time friend Jon Swanson. It was originally his grandmother's (Elizabeth Swanson) recipe.

2 C sweet potatoes, cooked* and mashed
1 C sugar or monk-fruit sweetener
1 t salt
2 C milk, warm
1 T melted butter
1 t. cinnamon
⅛ t. nutmeg
⅛ t. allspice

Mix all ingredients until of uniform consistency. Pour into unbaked pie shells. Bake at 350 for about 40 minutes. Serve warm and plain or with whipped cream.
 *you can cube and boil peeled sweet potatoes, but we have used baked leftover sweet potatoes with fair success.

PECAN & WALNUT PIE
3 eggs, well beaten
½ C sugar or monk fruit sweetener
1 C light or dark corn syrup
1 t. vanilla

¼ C butter, melted but not so hot that it will cook the eggs
1 oz. rum
½ C each chopped pecans and walnuts
½ C either chocolate chips OR Butterfinger chips

Mix all ingredients well until blended. Pour into unbaked pie shell and bake 30-35 minutes at 350 degrees until center is set. NOTE: if using chocolate/Butterfinger chips, omit sugar.

OATMEAL & PEANUT BUTTER COOKIES
(From Theresa)
I initially made this recipe for my students, to celebrate their Senior English final exam, May 2021. According to newspaper reports this particular spring, due to the China Coronavirus pandemic, only 24 percent of public-school students received in-person learning. My students were very appreciative to be among the 24 percent and not the 76 percent who missed out--and I was very glad to make something special for these deserving young people.

1 C peanut butter (I recommend whipped – especially not chunky)
1 C brown sugar, packed
2 eggs, beaten
2 ½ C oatmeal (quick cooking but NOT instant)
1 t. baking soda

Cream together PB & sugar until fluffy. Beat in eggs. Add oats and soda; mix well. Using a large spoon, drop two inches apart on greased cookie sheet. Using a spatula, flatten cookies slightly. Bake at 350 degrees for 6-8 minutes. Remove from oven, and let cool 5-10 minutes, then move them gently to a wire rack.

MOM'S BEST CHOCOLATE PIE
This recipe makes 2 pies, so cut ingredients by half if you only want one.

2/3 C AP flour
2 C sugar or monk fruit sweetener
2/3 C unsweetened cocoa
4 C water
¼ t. salt
6 eggs, separated
½ t. Cream of Tartar
1 stick butter, softened
2 t. vanilla
Two baked 9-10" deep dish pie shells

Sift together flour, sugar, cocoa & salt; place in large saucepan. Add water slowly, mixing well and stirring over low heat. Stir constantly until thickened. Remove from heat and mix tiny amount of hot mixture into yolks, then slowly add rest of yolks to mixture, stirring constantly. Add butter & vanilla and mix well. Pour equal amounts of mixture into the baked pie shells.

Beat egg whites and Cream of Tartar until stiff peaks form. Fold this (meringue) mixture onto tops of pies and spread to the edges of the pie crust to seal. Pop pies into the oven; bake at 350 degrees 6-8 minutes until meringue is golden. Remove from oven and cool on rack. Serve at room temperature. Refrigerate leftovers (if you have any!).

AUNT JOANN'S HEALTH COOKIES
(From Theresa)
My Aunt Joann Bagwell makes these for my Uncle Wendell. With all the butter and sugar in these, I'm not sure why she calls them "Health Cookies," but there you go!

¾ C butter, softened
½ C light brown sugar
1 t. vanilla
1 egg, beaten

Cream all these together, then whisk these (below) together and add to first four ingredients:

¾ C AP flour
½ t. each baking soda and powder*
1 t. cinnamon
1 t. salt

Then mix these together:

1 C *each* walnuts or pecans, chopped, raisins (golden), cranberries, coconut
5 C Old Fashioned Oatmeal

Mix nuts, raisins, cranberries, coconut and oatmeal well; add to the rest of the ingredients. Drop by tablespoons onto cookie sheet sprayed with non-stick. Bake at 350 degrees for 15-17 minutes. Cool & enjoy!

*If you use Self-Rising Flour for this recipe, omit baking soda and powder.

AUNT LILA'S APPLE CRUNCH
My sister-in-law, Lila Lacey Terry, made this for my first "married" birthday. Later, my kids liked it so much they would ask, "Make Aunt Lila's Apple Crunch!"

Peel and slice 6 to 7 medium apples, place in 2 qt. baking dish and add ½ cup of water. Sprinkle over top of apples with a mixture of ½ tsp cinnamon and ½ cup sugar, then sprinkle juice of one lemon over apples.

CRUMB TOPPING
Mix together 3/4 cup oatmeal, ½ tsp cinnamon, 1 cup sugar, ½ cup butter at room temp. Place over top of apples and don't try to spread it even.

Bake at 250-300° for 45-60 minutes. Top should be very bubbly and brown.
I have used peaches with this as well. Just add 1 tbsp of AP flour to the fruit.

AUNT LILA'S BLACKBERRY CRUNCH
> 1 C oatmeal
> 1 C flour
> Dash salt
> 1 stick butter, melted
> 2/3 C sugar
> 1 can blackberries, drained (or 2 cups fresh, washed)
> Cinnamon, lemon juice and/or vanilla

Mix all together, sprinkle cinnamon and sugar on top. Bake 350 until done.

FRUIT COBBLER
(From Theresa)
My mom was visiting for 2 ½ weeks in June of 2021, while my sister Mary and her husband Dean were on a trip to Colorado. The night of June 7, we had Sarah, Bo, Gus and Brandi over for a steak dinner. Sarah made some fried Silver Queen corn (see that recipe in the chapter on vegetables) to go with it, and Mom made some blackberry cobbler we had with ice cream for dessert. A rare treat! So here's the recipe specifically for blackberry cobbler. Adjust the sugar for sweeter fruits, such as peaches.

> 1 ½-2 pints fresh blackberries
> 1 C sugar or monk-fruit sweetener
> 1 C water
> 6 T butter
> 1 pie crust, cut into strips (we used Pillsbury)

Rinse blackberries; place 3-4 strips of pie crust in bottom of a rectangular baking dish (8 x 10 is what I used). Put blackberries on top of strips and sprinkle sugar over berries. Pour water over berries. Dot with butter and top with the rest of the pie crust slices.

Bake at 400 (preheated oven) for 30-45 minutes or until bubbly and crust is brown. If eating immediately, remove from oven and allow to "set" for about 10-15 minutes. If eating later, turn oven off and let the dessert sit in the oven until ready to enjoy. Best with vanilla ice cream.

GINGERBREAD
This is another of my mom's recipes. She says it goes great with coffee!

> 2 ⅓ C AP flour
> ½ C shortening (I recommend butter-flavored Crisco)
> ⅓ C sugar (optional, see note at end of recipe)
> 1 C molasses
> ¾ C hot water

1 t. each soda, ginger and cinnamon
¾ t. salt
2 eggs

Combine all ingredients in order given; blend well. Best with mixer on low speed for about one minute. Pour into well-greased and floured 13x9" pan. Bake in 350 degree oven about 45 minutes or until it passes the toothpick test.

*We made this, omitting the sugar, and it was plenty sweet. Let your taste buds be your guide!

DONNA'S APPLE CAKE
This is from a friend of my mom's, who just wanted to contribute something to the cookbook.

3 ½ C apples, peeled, cored & chopped
2 C SR flour
2 C sugar
3 large eggs, slightly beaten
¾ C veg. oil
1 t. each vanilla and cinnamon
½ t. cardamom
1 C walnuts, chopped

In mixer bowl, mix above ingredients *except apples* together until consistency is good. Stir in 2 C. SR flour, one cup at a time. Add 1 C. chopped walnuts. Finally, add the apples. Pour batter into a greased and floured tube (Bundt) pan. Bake at 350 degrees for 40-50 minutes until golden brown and it passes "the toothpick test." Cool in pan 10 minutes, then turn out onto serving plate. Sprinkle with powdered sugar. Best served warm.

MOM'S APPLE PIE
This is TRULY my "Mom's Apple Pie" recipe! She shared it with me June 2021.

6 medium Granny Smith apples (or your choice)
1/3 C brown sugar
1-2 t. cinnamon
1/3 C AP flour
½ stick butter, melted
2 pie crusts, with the bottom one baked a little

Peel, core and slice apples thinly. Pour melted butter over apples and toss. In small bowl, mix flour, sugar, salt and cinnamon together. Pour over apples and gently press down with fingers.

Pour fruit mixture into lightly baked bottom crust and put top crust on. Crimp edges; with knife, make small slices in crust. Bake 45-55 minutes on 350 until bubbly and crust is brown.

FRESH STRAWBERRY PIE
(From Theresa)

As a child growing up on my grandparents' farm in north Alabama, one of my favorite things to do in the summer was to go berry-picking with my brother, sisters, and cousins. There was nothing better back then than to pick fresh berries, especially strawberries, and then have my grandmother, mother or an aunt make this pie for supper.

    1 qt. strawberries, washed, drained and halved
    5 T. cornstarch
    1 C water
    1 C. sugar
    1 baked pie shell or one graham cracker crust

Cook cornstarch, sugar and water together until thick; boil one minute more. Then add 1 T butter. Fold in strawberries. Put berries in pre-baked pie shell.

Refrigerate until set. We recommend you serve with whipped cream. Good for a hot day!

PECAN-WALNUT PIE
    3 eggs, well beaten
    ½ C sugar or Monk-fruit sweetener
    1 C corn syrup (light or dark)
    1 t. vanilla
    ¼ C butter, melted
    1 oz rum
    1 unbaked pie shell
    ½ C EACH pecan and walnuts pieces
    ½ C chocolate chips OR Butterfinger pieces

Mix all ingredients until well blended. Pour into unbaked pie crust and bake 30-35 minutes at 350. It is done when it's set (not jiggly) in the center. NOTE: if using chocolate chips or Butterfinger pieces, omit sugar.

BUTTERMILK PIE
(From Theresa)
This recipe was created by my grandmother, Simmie Catherine Parker Bagwell. She had 12 children, so she was cooking something all the time.

    1 C sugar
    3 eggs, beaten
    3 T. AP flour
    ¼ C butter, melted
    1 C buttermilk
    1 t. lemon extract
    ½ C coconut (optional)
    1 unbaked pie shell

Blend eggs with sugar and flour. Add melted butter and beat well. Add buttermilk and lemon extract (and coconut if desired). Mix well.

Pour into unbaked pie shell and bake at 350 40-45 minutes or until crust is brown and pie is set.

LEMON-SOUR CREAM PIE
(From Theresa)
This is one of my dear friend's favorites. Debbie Swindell Flynt is as good a cook as she is an artist! She gave this to me written in narrative form, and I decided to keep it that way.

Combine 1 C sugar, 3 T cornstarch, and dash salt. Slowly stir in 1 C milk. Cook and stir 'til mixture is boiling and thickened. Blend small amount of hot mixture into 3 slightly beaten eggs; return to hot mixture. Cook and stir 2 minutes. Add 4 T butter, 1 t lemon zest and ¼ C lemon juice. Cover and let cool. Fold in 1 C sour cream. Spoon into baked pie shell. Top with meringue (below).

MERINGUE
Beat 3 egg whites with ¼ t cream of tartar and ½ t vanilla until soft peaks form. Gradually add 6 T sugar, beating to stiff peaks. Spread meringue over pie, sealing to edge. Bake at 350 for 12-15 minutes until golden brown.

Helpful hint from the author: when separating your eggs to make meringue, if even a *speck* of yolk gets in with the egg whites, they will not make peaks! If this happens, pour yolks and whites back together and refrigerate to make something else (omelets and such). Start with a fresh bowl and new eggs. This one I learned from experience.

SATSUMA MERINGUE PIE
(From Theresa)
In the Deep South of what we call "LA" (Lower Alabama), satsumas are a special treat in the wintertime. They're akin to oranges or tangerines, but have a rich, citrus taste all their own. When I first began experimenting with satsumas as a meringue pie, I made it too sweet initially. They have their own, natural sweetness, so here is what I (finally!) perfected.

1 baked pie crust
3 large egg yolks, slightly beaten
3/4 C sugar or monk-fruit sweetener
1/3 C plus 2 T cornstarch
1 ½ C water
3 T butter
2 t satsuma zest
½ C satsuma juice
Meringue for pie (see above recipe)

Heat oven to 400 degrees. In a saucepan, put sugar and cornstarch; gradually stir in water. Cook over medium heat, stirring constantly, until mixture thickens and boils. Boil and stir one additional minute. Take half of this mixture and add to egg yolks. Stir and add to saucepan with the rest of the mixture. Boil and stir 1-2 minutes. Add satsuma zest, butter, and satsuma juice. Pour into pie crust.

Make meringue as directed in the preceding recipe and pour over hot satsuma pie filling. Make sure you seal the edges with the meringue. Bake at 400 degrees for about 10-12 minutes or until meringue is light brown. Remove from oven and cool away from draft. Once cooled, cover and refrigerate until ready to serve. Another lesson we learned: the meringue will pull away from the sides if the pie cools in an otherwise humid environment (this won't affect the taste or the consistency, but it won't be as visually appealing). Perhaps turn off the oven and let it cool gradually.

HUMMINGBIRD CAKE
This is my friend Rachel Swanson's recipe.

3 C AP flour
1 t baking soda
½ t. salt
2 C sugar
1 t. cinnamon
3 eggs, beaten
¾ C vegetable oil
1 ½ t vanilla extract
1 8 oz. can crushed pineapple, drained
1 C chopped pecans
1 ¾ C mashed ripe bananas (4-5)
½ C pecans, chopped
Cream Cheese Frosting

Combine first 5 ingredients; add eggs but do not beat. Stir in vanilla, pineapple, 1 C pecans & bananas. Pour batter into 3 greased cake pans. Bake at 350 for 23-28 minutes or until toothpick inserted comes out clean. When cool, frost with your favorite Cream Cheese frosting.

SOUTHERN STYLE ENGLISH SCONES

(From Theresa)

Back in the 19th century, some of my people immigrated from England. That may make them sound very proper, but many of them were proverbial salt of the earth–laborers such as carpenters and coal-miners. One dish my grandmother showed me how to make was scones. Not exactly a cookie, many a scone found its way into my ancestors' lunch buckets. This is another thing my grandmother let me watch her making.

⅓ C stick butter, softened
1 ¼ C SRF
½ c\C oats, quick-cooking
3 T honey or sugar
2 t grated lemon peel
1 large egg, beaten
½ C golden raisins, cranberries or other fruit
4-6 T half & half
1 large egg, beaten

Heat oven to 400. In a large mixing bowl, cut butter into flour, oats and lemon peel. Mix until blended and appearance is that of meal. Add egg, raisins and half & half, just enough until dough leaves sides of bowl.

Turn dough onto lightly floured cutting board and knead about 1 minute. Roll out into ½ inch thickness. Cut using a biscuit cutter and place onto ungreased cookie sheet. Brush with beaten egg.

Bake 10-12 minutes until golden brown on top. Remove scones to cooling rack. Good warm. Keeps for a few days at room temperature.

CHAPTER 7

EGG & CHEESE DISHES

This is one of Jeanne Franklin Lacey's (Eric's Mom's) recipes.

BAKED MACARONI & CHEESE
Prepare 12 oz pkg macaroni, rinse in cold water. Butter a 2 qt casserole dish and set aside. Melt ½ stick of butter in saucepan. Stir in 4 tbsp plain flour until smooth. Blend in 1 ½ C whole milk, 1 ½ t. salt, ¼ t. pepper. Stir until sauce thickens, keep stirring as the sauce may stick to bottom of saucepan before you know it. Add 6 oz. sliced sharp cheddar cheese and stir until melted. Combine with cooked macaroni in the greased casserole dish. Sprinkle top with buttered breadcrumbs and parmesan cheese. Dot top with butter and bake in a 350° oven for 20 minutes. This dish freezes well.

A NOTE ON MAKING PERFECT, EASILY PEEL-ABLE BOILED EGGS

Try this boiled-egg method and you may never fight with an eggshell again! Start with placing the eggs in a saucepan of COLD water, where the water just covers the eggs. Cover; on LOW heat, slowly bring the water to a low boil (you cover it so, when the lid is jiggling, you know you've got a low boil going). Turn heat off but leave the cover on the pan. Set your timer for 25 minutes, as the eggs cook to a perfect turn. Then drain the water; place the eggs in a shallow bowl in the refrigerator for 2-3 hours or overnight. When you're ready to peel them, the eggshells will come off, and no "whites" will be wasted! Now you're ready to make deviled eggs.

T. Jensen Lacey

DINNER-ON-THE-GROUNDS DEVILED EGGS

(From Theresa)

Every Memorial Day weekend, my people would gather at our family cemetery in north Alabama. We'd clean and decorate the gravesites and tombstones of those who'd gone before. After we were finished, we'd share a meal, where everybody brought something. This deviled egg recipe has been in my family for generations, but variations, influenced by family members with "other" backgrounds and cultures, are below.

    12 eggs, boiled, cooled, and peeled
    1 C mayonnaise
    2 T lemon juice (or more, to your liking)
    Salt and pepper to taste
    ¼ C Dill relish
    Paprika

Slice the eggs in half; gently scoop out the cooked yolk into a mixing bowl. Place the cooked whites on a deviled egg tray, open side up. Mix the yolks with the mayonnaise, lemon juice, S&P and dill relish. Add more mayonnaise if it's not creamy enough to your liking. Dust with paprika. Keep chilled and covered until ready to serve.

VARIATIONS: Use Tony Chachere's to add a Cajun flavor. Substitute sweet relish for dill, or mix it half and half, for a sweeter flavor. Add 1 can (drained and chopped) water chestnuts for a crunchy, Asian twist, or add ¼ C chopped celery. Add ¼ C finely diced sweet onion. Use Smoked Paprika for a greater depth of flavor. You may also substitute (plain) Greek yogurt for mayonnaise. Any way you make these, you are guaranteed to come home with an empty serving dish.

SALUTE TO SEUSS! GREEN EGGS & HAM

(From Theresa)

It was back around 1998 when both my kids, Sarah and Gus, were in elementary school. They were celebrating Dr. Seuss at school, and one book we were reading was *Green Eggs and Ham*. I experimented a bit, and discovered that, when mixed with purple grape jelly, the eggs become green! The kids loved it. Note: it's strange, but you will not taste the grape jelly, just the eggs and ham. A chemist could explain all this.

    4 eggs, slightly beaten
    2 slices ham steak, cubed
    2 T butter, unsalted
    2-3 t purple grape jelly

Melt butter on medium heat in skillet. Add ham and cook until hot. Stir in eggs and jelly and watch the eggs (and ham!) magically become green!

THERESA'S QUICHE

I adore quiche! It's oftentimes a one-dish meal; it freezes well and can safely sit at room temperature for several hours, so you can carry it in a lunch bag and enjoy it at work or school.

For a basic quiche:

> 1 baked pie shell
> 1 pkg. real bacon bits OR 8 slices bacon, cooked and crumbled
> 1 C shredded cheese—depending on the flavor, use Swiss for a mild flavor or Cheddar for something stronger
> 1/3 C onion (I use Vidalia), finely chopped
> 4 large eggs
> 2 C heavy cream or ½ and ½
> Salt, pepper and cayenne to your liking

Preheat oven to 425. Into lightly baked pie shell, sprinkle bacon, cheese and onion. Beat eggs with cream and seasonings and pour over dry ingredients. Bake 15 minutes. Reduce oven to 300 degrees. Bake about a half-hour longer or until it is "set" in the center. Let rest 10 minutes before cutting.

To add variety to this basic quiche, you may add mushrooms, chopped; cooked shrimp; drained spinach (for more of a Quiche Lorraine), or a myriad of other variations.

Note: Eric likes to "sweat" the vegetables--especially onions, bell peppers, mushrooms--so that they aren't crunchy. "Sweating" as a culinary term that means, according to Betty Crocker's International Cookbook, "to cook using gentle heat in a little oil or butter, with frequent stirring and turning to ensure that emitted liquid will evaporate, often resulting in tender and sometimes translucent vegetables."

ENGLISH CLASS HASH BROWN CASSEROLE

(From Theresa)

The last 17 years of my teaching career, I taught High School English at Robertsdale High School in south Alabama. Those were probably my most stressful, yet most rewarding, years, because I found I could have a rapport with students who were in truth young adults.

I found that food is a great motivator, and every few weeks I would give a class a Good Behavior celebration. This was one of their favorite dishes. Note on hash brown placement: by pressing the browns in the bottom and sides of the casserole dish, they will bake up very crisp, not limp like you might think they would turn out.

For one casserole oblong dish, this serves 12-16 teenagers.

> One large package seasoned and frozen hash brown potatoes, thawed
> 18 eggs, lightly beaten
> 1 12-ounce package cheddar cheese, shredded

  1 12-ounce carton cream
  1 4.3 ounce package bacon bits

In glass casserole dish (roughly 9x13) sprayed with non-stick, press thawed hash browns into bottom and sides (as evenly as possible). In large mixing bowl, mix eggs, cheese, cream and bacon bits until well-blended. Pour into casserole dish on top of hash browns. Bake in a 375 degree preheated oven for about an hour or until set in the center.

CHAPTER 8

FISH AND SHELLFISH

Let's talk seafood:

Even living on the coast, unless we caught the fish within a day or so, we froze it – generally. Unless you are at the boat when they unload – and it is a smaller bay shrimper, all the shrimp nowadays are "IQF" (Individually Quick Frozen). It isn't a bad thing. You can literally pull out 6 shrimp from the freezer, thaw them in a colander with some cool water and have shrimp 24/7/365. IQF peeled and deveined shrimp (USA source ONLY) are great and we use them a lot in recipes. In my experience, the only drawback is if you are preparing boiled shrimp – then peeled and deveined doesn't seem to work as well.

There's Bay white shrimp – my favorite – usually harvested in the late fall (Nov/Dec).

There's also good 'ol gray shrimp – the base of the whole food chain.

There's also Royal Reds – these shrimp live in deep water (over 200 feet) and are reddish color. The taste is like lobster – a little sweet and rich. They are also usually big (10-15 count is normal). They are great boiled. Also good grilled.

Most commercially-harvested fish are the same, and the quality is preserved for enjoyment at your convenience. After a snapper trip, we will keep out some filets for consumption in the next day or two – the rest are frozen right away.

I've tried oysters frozen/thawed. In my experience, don't do it. Frozen crab meat – if it is going into a gumbo or au gratin it's OK, but as a topping or crab cake it doesn't really work so well – it's mushy and the texture just doesn't seem to work.

While on the topic, I've included the family boiled shrimp recipe – it is simple, and delivers consistent, peelable, flavorful shrimp every time.

BOILED SHRIMP – LA (Lower Alabama) LOW COUNTRY STYLE WITH COCKTAIL SAUCE

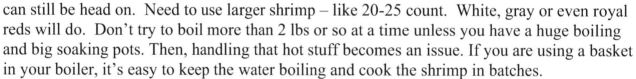

The basic process is to boil the shrimp, briefly, then remove the shrimp from the hot water and put them in a cold water "soak." Even if you didn't use any of the spices, this method will achieve perfectly cooked, well peeling shrimp.

Depending on how many you are feeding, this is scalable. Make sure the shrimp are not peeled; they can still be head on. Need to use larger shrimp – like 20-25 count. White, gray or even royal reds will do. Don't try to boil more than 2 lbs or so at a time unless you have a huge boiling and big soaking pots. Then, handling that hot stuff becomes an issue. If you are using a basket in your boiler, it's easy to keep the water boiling and cook the shrimp in batches.

Note: crab boil, when boiling will cause you to sneeze – a lot. If you can, add the crab boil just before adding any items and if inside, turn on the exhaust fan and open a window. You may get criticized by non-participants, but they will get over it when they enjoy the fruits of your labor.

If you have some help, get them to make some cocktail sauce while you work on your shrimp art. Recipe below:

COCKTAIL SAUCE

    1 ½ cups good (not sweet) ketchup (we like Whataburger spicy ketchup)
    2 T fresh horseradish (not "prepared" or "horseradish sauce" – real ground horseradish
    – can be found in refrigerated section of most grocery stores)

Couple dashes of Worcestershire sauce
Couple dashes of tabasco
Lemon juice to taste

Mix well, keep adding from ingredients till you get the taste you want. We would normally use more horseradish than this, but that's just us.

Some folks like drawn butter with lemon on the side. Really no way to mess these up if you follow the directions.

BOILING THE SHRIMP
2 big pots: 1 for boiling and 1 for soaking.
(FYI for about $100 you can get a King Kooker set up with a propane burner, a big boiling pot, and smaller boiling pot with a perforated basket , which makes life very easy)

2 lbs of fresh shrimp, as noted – if they still have heads on, add 1/3.
Zatarain's liquid crab boil (about 4 T for boiling, about 2 T for soaking)
3 T kosher salt (2 T for boiling, 1 T for soaking)
Handful of bay leaves
A few sprigs of fresh rosemary
2-3 lemons, washed and sliced in half
1 lb BB or BBB red jacket potatoes
1 lb Conecuh sausage
2 bags of ice

Set up big pot, fill it 2/3 full of water, add 2 T salt, the bay leaves and rosemary.

Set up soaking pot: fill it 2/3 full of *cold* tap water, add 1 T salt and 2 T crab boil; stir well to mix.

Bring big pot to a boil. Add 4 T Crab Boil. If you have a basket, put potatoes in basket and add to boiling pot. Check potatoes after 10 minutes. When soft but not mushy, remove potatoes and set aside. Add Conecuh sausage and return to boil. Cut lemons in half and squeeze into boiling pot.

Put spent lemon halves in the soaking pot.

Immediately add shrimp. Stir frequently to blend shrimp – this is not the time to go get a beer. After 3 minutes, dip a shrimp out of the boiling pot and put in soaking pot. Wait a minute then remove that test shrimp and peel it and eat it. If it isn't quite done, remove another test shrimp and repeat. As soon as the test shrimp meat is firm and it peels easily, turn off boiler, remove shrimp immediately and place in cold water to soak. While the shrimp are soaking, fish out the sausage and set aside with the potatoes.

After about 5 minutes in the soak, remove the shrimp and cover them with a layer of cracked ice. Blend/mix (use both hands) in the ice with the shrimp. You want them to cool off/chill quickly. Leave a layer of ice on top of shrimp.

I serve the shrimp in a colander in a bowl and dump out any melted ice/shrimp water when it accumulates.

Serve the shrimp slightly chilled, and the potatoes and sausage still warm.

To keep any uneaten shrimp, you can remove heads and place shrimp in a Zip-loc bag in the fridge for a day or two. If you want them to disappear, peel them first and the lazy snackers will eliminate them – or you can use them in an omelet or shrimp salad.

BOILED BLUE CRABS

To boil blue crabs, you will use the same procedure as shrimp, however, you don't need a soaking pot. If cooking raw (not frozen/prepped crabs) if the crab is dead, DISCARD. When you remove the crabs from the trap, if in doubt, toss him out.

You can do this with clusters and claws previously harvested, cleaned and frozen.

Get the boiler with salt, crab boil, herbs, and lemon to a high boil. Place crabs in the pot one at a time. When full (will hold 12 or so crabs), stir around gently and place lid on. Return to rolling boil and cook about 8 minutes. Turn off boiler; remove crabs from pot and scatter on newspaper and let them drain and cool.

When they have cooled enough to be handled, begin by removing carapace, break into 2 clusters, scooping out that yellow stuff, and start teasing out the meat from the clusters. Crack the claws with a cracker or pliers. Forget the hammer – just makes a huge mess. I use a toothpick to tease out the meat.

Some folks like to coat the boiled crabs with Old Bay or Chachere's – there is no bad way to enjoy them. I like to dredge the meat in drawn butter.

GAMBAS EN AJILLO (SHRIMP IN GARLIC)

While in Spain I love to feast on tapas. We make larger batches of this at my house and eat it right out of the pan, "tribal style." So good – so simple and so quick.

Apx 2 dozen 20-25 count shrimp peeled (IQF peeled and deveined works great – thawed first and drained)
Half a stick of butter
¼ C olive oil
6 large cloves garlic, smashed and diced
1 large lemon, halved

Prepare raw peeled shrimp (thaw if frozen, drain, let stand).

In a large cast iron skillet, heat olive oil and butter to high temp (almost smoking). Add garlic and shrimp, stirring constantly for about 4 minutes – making sure to cook both sides of each shrimp.

Remove from heat. Eat!

I serve it on my kitchen island with toothpicks and French bread for dredging that wonderful, buttery sauce.

If you have more shrimp and hungry people, you can repeat with what's left in the skillet, adding a bit more butter, garlic and oil before adding the shrimp. We've never had leftovers to discuss.

ITALIAN-STYLE SHRIMP WITH HERBS AND ANDOUILLE.

Brown one lb. andouille sausage cut diagonally. The last few minutes add 1/8 cup of olive oil. Remove sausage; drain and reserve liquid. Add oil back to the pan. On medium heat brown 4 minced cloves of garlic and one 6-inch sprig of rosemary in the oil. Drain and reserve liquid.

Return oil to pan. Saute approx. ½ of a medium sweet onion, chopped, ½ of a medium red bell pepper, chopped, and ½ of a green and yellow bell pepper, also chopped. Also add a handful of white mushrooms, chopped, to the oil. Put in skillet and sauté until soft.

Add 1 lb. peeled white (deveined if sand-line is prominent) shrimp (I use 20-25#), until lightly pink on both sides. Add sausage. Add ½ cup dry white wine; stir thoroughly. Add one can diced tomatoes, drained. Bring to a boil and simmer for about 5 minutes. Turn off then add back the garlic and rosemary and 5 heads of basil, 4 leaves of sage, and a long run of fresh oregano, all diced. Toss and serve. We had this with rice. Excellent!

ERIC'S CABBAGE, SHRIMP AND PEANUT STIR-FRY WITH FISH

Eric cooked this the night of November 14, 2019. It was just the two of us, thus, a good night to experiment. It was fantastic!

Chop the following for stir fry:
> ½ cabbage head, then quartered, then slice vertically so it's chopped. Discard the thick veins near the base.
> 1 C salted peanuts, chopped
> ¼ Vidalia onion, finely cut

In a small bowl, combine 1 cup creamy or whipped peanut butter, 2 T Rice Wine Vinegar, 1 tsp minced garlic, 2 T soy sauce, juice of half a lime and ½ pound peeled, fresh, white bay shrimp. Toss mixture together and add a big dash of pepper. Let sit for a while.

Prepare the fish:
Before cooking, start with a little marinade: use the juice of half a lime, a quarter stick butter melted, add a bit of chopped, sun-dried tomatoes and basil (fresh is always best). Place fish in a

prep dish and coat both sides with the marinade. If skin is still on, put meat side down. Let sit about an hour.

Preheat oven to 350 degrees, Place cast iron skillet with small amount of veg oil (Wesson) in oven until oil is hot. Place filets, skin side down, and move filets around so they don't stick. Add marinade to coat filets.

Bake filets at 350 until done (flake w a fork). Depending on thickness of filets – seldom more than 10 minutes. Baste at 5 minutes and check for doneness.

Stir-fry the cabbage while the fish are baking. Place cabbage stir fry on heated plate with fish filet on top.

This Stir-fry can be served alone as its own dish – served with rice is nice!

GUMBO
(From Eric)

Growing up and living on the Gulf Coast, one gets to sample lots of gumbo – unfortunately, so many times it is 'way too salty.

Other times, not enough attention to the roux creates either a gravy that's a soup-like consistency, or worse, a burnt tasting experiment. There are a few secrets that are tried-and-true, based on extensive field testing, and totally satisfactory. If you have an extra hour or so to start a roux from scratch, I suggest a 50/50 mix of bacon fat and Wesson vegetable oil, heated almost right up to the smoke point, stirring constantly as you whisk or fork in a teaspoon of AP flour a T at a time until it gets to a rich, dark yet still liquid consistency. If it smells burned, discard and start over. I never seem to make enough – or too much – and it will freeze, but that's another Ziploc bag of mystery stuff in the freezer. I prefer to use jarred roux – I can add all I need, balancing the flavor and color of the gumbo, and save the 1 ½ hour of prep time. Heated debates will always rage over okra/no okra. I say – add it if you want – I eat it that way if served, but I don't cook it that way. If you have ever had slimy gumbo and had gone to all the trouble to make it, then you understand.

This particular recipe serves 10-15. You can stretch it with an extra can of diced tomatoes and 1 C water. There isn't a reasonable way to make a small amount, however, it freezes very well.

You will need:

1 aprox 2 lbs whole chicken (can use just thighs)
1 lb Conecuh sausage (most preferred) – can substitute southern style or Andouille – just not Italian style
1 medium Vidalia onion, chopped
1 medium green bell pepper, washed and chopped
4 stalks of celery, same way
Fresh oregano – 2 or 3 sprigs
Fresh Rosemary – 2 sprigs
Bay leaves
Salt (very little!)
Black pepper
1 can diced tomatoes
1 ½ - 2 lbs peeled shrimp. I like 20-25 count.
1 pint oysters with liquid
1-2 medium fish filets (I like trigger, redfish – even bee liner snapper) If you don't have it – OK to skip. Do not use salmon or tuna.
3-4 crabs, cleaned (clusters with no fins/flippers) – crack the claws before adding if available
Roux: I use "Kary's" in the jar – you will see why

For serving:
White rice (prefer jasmine)
Tabasco
Chachere's
Gumbo Filet

In a 6 quart stock pot, place whole chicken (I include innards if they come with the bird), just covered in water with 1 T salt, 1 T black pepper, 4-5 Bay Leaves, 2 sprigs rosemary, 2 sprigs oregano. Cover, bring to a boil and let simmer for 30+ minutes. You are making the stock for the gumbo and will remove the bones and cartilage from the stock when the chicken is fully cooked/falling off the bone.

In a Dutch oven, place sausage chopped into ½" pieces and saute, covered, until mostly cooked. Remove sausage, reserving grease. Put chopped onion, celery and bell pepper into Dutch oven and add back the sausage grease as needed to "sweat" the veggies. Add the can of tomatoes; return the sausage to Dutch oven and simmer on low.

When chicken is done and cool enough to handle, debone and replace into stock. Add chicken and stock to Dutch oven and keep simmering on low. Adjust liquid amount by sight – it's OK to add a cup of water – sometimes another can of diced tomatoes – depending on how many you will feed.

Now the magic: To the pot, at a low simmer, add (a tablespoon at a time) the roux, mixing well each time and tasting. What you want is a darker overall appearance and slightly thicker, smoky flavor (not burned!!!). I usually end up adding 4-5 T. This needs to come to a simmer for an hour or so. DO NOT ADD SALT IN ANY FORM. Stir frequently to prevent roux from settling on the bottom and burning. If that happens, throw it all away. It cannot be saved/salvaged. Adding further ingredients just wastes them.

For best results, remove from heat and let cool, covered, to almost room temp.

After cooling (especially good if reheated next day or from frozen), gently bring gumbo back to a very low simmer, stirring frequently. Add crab bodies and continue simmering about 30 minutes, stirring, stirring, tasting. About 15 minutes before serving, add shrimp, oysters and fish, stirring gently. As soon as shrimp are firm and oysters show their lips, turn off heat and serve.

The finish:
Rice: many serve gumbo over rice. I say make enough gumbo so you don't have to do that – serve rice on the side. Use Chachere's to add salty flavor to your OWN bowl of gumbo. I also add tabasco and a pinch of gumbo file to my bowl. NEVER add salt or Chachere's or especially file to the entire pot. That can be disastrous. "To each his own" is how I approach salt in almost every finished dish. When reheated, file will change in flavor and ruin the gumbo. Trust me, I've made all of these mistakes. I've even had folks try to slip in some salt or other seasoning while it is cooking – keep an eye on those sorts of people – they can't be trusted and will steal from you too.

The fish, crab, shrimp and especially the oysters all add natural salty/umami flavor. The delicacy of each critter's flavor comes through without further ingredients added to the pot. Over-spicing ruins most gumbo. The flavor comes from each ingredient – not the spices. This isn't taco meat.

Legacy of gumbo: As long as you get the shrimp, oysters and crab out of it, gumbo reheats very well – within a few days of cooking. It is actually preferable to make gumbo ahead of time, chill overnight in the fridge and reheat gently. Otherwise, seal in a Ziploc, removing all air and freeze. I've had gumbo from a year ago and it was excellent. Just add seafood like noted at the end of reheating – stirring, stirring, stirring. Or if you are latitudinally challenged, chicken and sausage gumbo is just fine. I've made the same basic gumbo using sausage, pheasant and rabbit (very good); sausage and wild duck is good (my old friend Porter King used ducks like pouldeau or scaup). In the end, it's "what you got."

OYSTERS LACEY
Eric first perfected this in the fall of 2017. We serve it piping hot with crusty warm French bread (or even grilled tortillas). Even people who say they don't like oysters LOVE this! Use a muffin tin or ramekins if you have a bunch and don't mind all the handling. We usually gather around the end of the island in the kitchen and use spoons and bread – tailgate family style. (Tribal style, T calls it)

Recipe makes enough for a 12-hole muffin tin (1 round, we call it).

> Pint of fresh shucked oysters
> Thai chili garlic (Sriracha is my fave)
> Lemon
> Butter
> Parmesan
> Bread crumbs
> French bread for dredging

Count your oysters and see how big they are. Put them in a strainer and adjust your recipe accordingly.

In a ramekin, put half a stick of unsalted butter, 2 T of Sriracha/Thai Chili Garlic Sauce, the juice of half a lemon; pop this in the microwave until it's melted. Mix well.

In a muffin-tin (for 12 muffins), spray with no-stick; put an even amount of the melted butter and chili sauce into the cups. Preheat oven to 425. When mixture bubbles, pull it out.

Put an even amount of oysters in each of the 12 tins. Toss to coat with chili sauce mixture. Put back in oven and bake for approximately 8 minutes or until it starts to bubble again.

Meanwhile, take 1/2 cup of plain breadcrumbs and ½ cup Parmesan cheese. Mix thoroughly. After the oysters bubble, remove from oven. Put an equal amount of cheese mixture in each cup and toss gently to coat. Put back in the oven for about 5 minutes, then put on High Broil for 3-4 minutes until Parmesan cheese topping browns. Serve "Tribal Style" where everybody eats from the muffin tins.

SAVORY SALMON

We created this on a day after we'd had four days of rain; boredom had set in, along with cabin fever, so we decided to get experimental in the kitchen. We made it 4-18-2021.

> 2 filets fresh salmon
> 2 T soy sauce, minced fresh ginger
> 1 t of chili pepper
> 1 t dill
> Juice of half a lemon
> 2 whole turnips, peeled and chopped
> 2 T butter
> A dash of Chachere's

Lightly coat salmon with Chachere's and melted butter; set aside and let salmon come to room temp (about an hour).

Combine all other ingredients.
Preheat oven to 400. Coat a cast-iron skillet with bacon fat and olive oil. Add turnips; toss in oil and roast for 20 min. Add salmon to skillet, arranging turnips around salmon and bake 'til thermometer registers at 145 degrees.

KATHERINE AINSWORTH'S SEAFOOD CASSEROLE

Katherine Ainsworth was our friend Jon Swanson's grandmother, and this was one of his favorite dishes as a child.

> 4 C bread-cubes (about 6 slices)
> 1 8-ounce salmon filet, flaked (in a pinch, you can use a can of tuna or salmon, drained)
> 1 C *each* onion, celery, and green bell pepper, all chopped
> 2 C mayonnaise
> 4 eggs, lightly beaten
> 2 C milk
> 1 can cream of mushroom soup
> ½ C sharp cheddar cheese, shredded

Put half of the bread cubes in bottom of a greased casserole dish. Mix fish, onion, celery, pepper and mayonnaise and spread over bread cubes. Top with remaining half of the bread cubes. In a bowl, mix milk, soup and eggs and pour over what's in casserole dish. Top with shredded cheese.

Bake at 350 degrees for about an hour. This dish serves about 6 people.

ERIC'S ETOUFFEE

Eric cooked this April 22, 2020. We were in quarantine due to the Coronavirus and this was our sixth week. We thought then (and were told) that this would be the end-all—that this mass quarantine would "flatten the curve." So we spent a lot of time experimenting in the kitchen.

> 1 pound peeled deveined royal reds, 25-30 ct
> 2 big cloves garlic, smashed and minced
> Tablespoon each olive oil and butter
> dash each Tony's (Chachere's), black pepper
> ½ C of dry white wine
> 1 pkg. Goya tomato stock concentrate
> ½ C boiling water
> ½ C each sour cream and cream cheese, both at room temperature
> Italian seasoning
> dash fried garlic

Put the peeled shrimp in a 2 qt bowl. Let them come to room temperature. Squirt with a teaspoon lemon juice and toss.

Heat butter and olive oil in skillet; add minced garlic. Brown garlic, stirring constantly. Remove from heat and strain, reserving both garlic and oil/butter mixture.

Let the butter/olive oil cool slightly. Add approx. a teaspoon of the butter/olive oil and Tony's to the shrimp and toss. Let marinate 30 minutes or so.

Take ½ box good spaghetti, boiled, drained and set aside. Saute shrimp approx. 2 minutes per side.

Turn off heat, remove shrimp. Add one pkg. Sauzon Goya tomato stock concentrate in ½ cup boiling water. Add to skillet.

Turn fire on medium; bring to a boil. Reduce by half. Add 1 T. or more sour cream; stir and blend. Add a half-cup of white French table wine and reduce by half. Add a T cream cheese; blend thoroughly. Add another splash white wine.

Let this sauce thicken while stirring constantly. Once to desired thickness, add shrimp and juice back. Stir to coat.

Turn off heat and cover. Let sit for 5 minutes. Meanwhile, heat plates, put pasta bed down, spoon it up, dust with fried garlic and enjoy.

BASIC COURTBOUILLON (Quick and easy, recommended for beginners)

We are blessed to have a number of Cajuns in our family. Dustin LeBlanc, a nephew, and Bill Terry, a brother-in-law, are both very adept at making this classic Cajun dish (pronounced Coo-Bee-Yahn). Dustin will make this with whatever frozen fish he has that needs to be used, as will Bill Terry. From what I understand, you can use just about any fish, frozen or fresh, with the exception of catfish or trout, due to problems with the consistency (the finished product will be mushy).

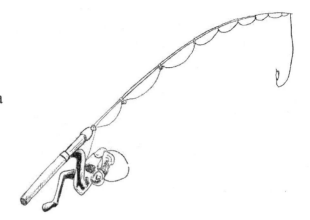

    5 lb fresh or frozen fish, such as Red Snapper (boned and cubed)
    2 lbs Irish potatoes, washed and thinly sliced

    In baking pan put a layer of potatoes and fish, repeating layers until pan is full. Make this sauce and pour over fish and potatoes.
    SAUCE
    2 cans diced tomatoes (do not drain)
    1 C onions, chopped
    1 bell pepper, chopped
    3 bay leaves
    Dash of garlic, salt and pepper

Bake at 275 degrees for about an hour. This goes well with a side of garlic-cheese grits and cornbread.

SHO-NUFF COURTBOUILLON (Long cut, for seasoned chefs)
When time is available, this recipe is what Eric uses. It's more involved than the one above, but many of you will be up to the challenge!

Dark Roux (see Chapter 12 for that recipe, or use your own or Kary's jarred roux)
    2 large onions, sliced
    1 large can diced tomatoes, undrained
    1 large fish filet (Red Snapper, Amberjack, etc.), cubed
    2 bay leaves
    ¼ t allspice
    1 t parsley
    4 green bell peppers, sliced thinly
    4 shallots, chopped fine
    3clove garlic, sliced
    1 C dry red wine (a good Bourgogne or claret will do)
    1 C water
    Dash each salt and pepper

½ lemon, washed and sliced thinly

Saute onions in a tablespoon or so of bacon grease until translucent. Add canned tomatoes and cook 5 minutes. After 5 minutes, immediately add all other ingredients except for the fish. Add roux until desired consistency, flavor and color are achieved. After about 20-25 minutes, add the fish. Simmer slowly, covered, until fish is cooked and you are ready to serve. Good over rice.

RED SNAPPER PARMESAN

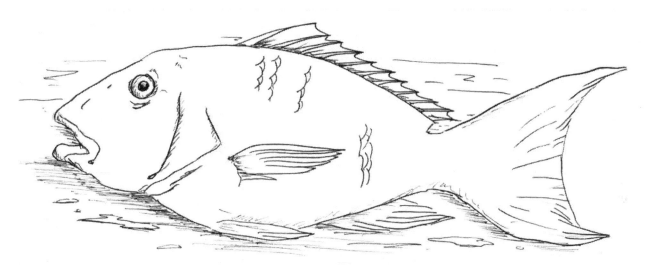

This recipe Eric cooked after one day of excellent fishing for Red Snapper in 2007. The fresher the fish you can get, the better this dish is. You can also try making this with Amberjack, white trout or flounder.

2 lbs Red Snapper filets
1 C sour cream
¼ C Parmesan cheese (not powdered—grated)
1-2 T lemon juice
1 T onion, grated
Dash each salt, Crystal hot sauce and smoked paprika

Let fish sit at room temperature for about 30 minutes. Remove skin from snapper filets and cut into serving size portions. In a well-greased baking dish (we used a 12x8), place the filets in a single layer. Combine all other ingredients except the paprika; spread this mixture over filets. Sprinkle top with the smoked paprika. Bake at 350 for 25-30 minutes until the thickest part of filets flake. This recipe served 6 hungry and happy anglers.

ERIC'S INTERPRETATION OF POP'S OYSTER STEW
Eric made this the night of 12-6-20, after a day of fishing with our son Gus. They began reminiscing about oysters, and how Pop/Granddaddy made great oyster stew. Way back in the '70's, Pop was City Attorney for Bayou La Batre. The mayor's wife used to make this for Pop

when he came down for City Council meetings. It became Pop's favorite. It's simple, but outstanding. Timing is the key.

    1 stick butter
    ½ Vidalia onion, minced
    16 oz fresh oysters
    ¼ t each salt and pepper
    Tabasco
    2 C half and half

Place minced onion and stick of butter in a 4 qt saucepan. Melt butter under medium heat and saute onion until clear. Add 1 cup half and half and continue to stir. Add oysters with juice from containers. Heat gently. At no point should this bubble and boil!

Stir frequently until the oyster lips vein or firm. Add the final cup half and half, balancing flavor with black pepper. If it needs salt, let each salt their own bowl. Serve immediately with good French bread and tabasco.

AUSTIN'S COBIA
Our late nephew Austin loved catching cobia because he said it was like hunting, but with a boat. Cobia is a seasonal top-water fish and really fun to catch. He said it was like bass-fishing in a 50-foot Hatteras.

We cooked this after running into Fairhope Fish Company's booth at the Farmers' Market on May 27, 2021.

    1-1/2 pounds Cobia tail, very fresh, cleaned
    2 T butter, olive oil
    Splash soy sauce
    1 T lemon juice

In a pan, combine butter, olive oil, etc. and place filet meat side down, skin side up (so you soak the meat in marinade). Meanwhile, prepare the grill to about 350 degrees. Spray with non-stick. Place filets on grill; smoke/grill until almost flaky. If your grill is not hot enough, pop filet(s) in oven at 425 until they're opaque all the way through.

Place on heated plates, dividing the filets or crosscutting the filets where the diner can remove the bloodline in the center.
Suggestion: serve with a little rice, grits, mashed potatoes, etc., in the middle to soak up the juice. We finished this one in the oven.

This recipe served the two of us, so increase accordingly.

ERIC'S FISH FILETS/PDQ MEUNIERE

This is an old standby that we've used for decades. We've used this for Red Snapper to Rainbow Trout and just about every other fish in between. Excellent with Gulf Gray Triggerfish filets (one of our favorites).

        1½ lbs fresh fish
        Black pepper
        1 C SR flour
        2 T lemon juice
        Olive oil, enough to cook what fish you've got
        2-3 T unsalted butter
        ¼ C good French white table wine, such as La Vieille Ferme
        Dash or two of Chachere's

Place filets in a shallow pan and squirt with lemon juice. Let stand as they come to room temperature. Place an equal amount of butter and olive oil in frying pan and bring to temp - not much - just about 2 T of butter and 2T of oil. Lightly coat filets with Chachere's, brush filets with melted butter/oil from pan. Lightly dust filets with self-rising flour. Put fish in skillet and brown on both sides; remove from skillet, transfer filets to an oven-proof plate and put in oven to keep warm.

Deglaze the skillet with white wine. Add more butter if needed; balance with lemon juice. Serve with rice or grits.

Variations and additions:

Louis: At the end, when the meuniere is done, add some fresh crab meat (lump is best) and toss lightly, serve immediately over fish.

Skipper King: to the meuniere, add 2 T of horseradish and 2 T of capers, toss to blend, serve over fish immediately. If using this variation, don't put Chachere's on filets (too salty in the end).

NANA'S SALMON CROQUETTES
(From Theresa)
I remember growing up with having salmon croquettes. We had it about once a week, especially when my family of 4 kids and two parents moved in with Grandmother, who wanted to keep the farm after Granddad's passing. We were then joined by my Aunt Juanee and her three kids. The cooks had to really stretch the protein to feed all those kids! Mom/Nana always served this with macaroni and cheese (see Chapter 8 for that recipe) and homemade coleslaw (see Chapter 13). This recipe goes back to the mid-1950s, so it's stood the proverbial test of time.

This recipe feeds 12, just like Grandmother and Mom cooked it on our farm in north Alabama.

3 cans salmon, drained (reserve liquid*), with bones picked out
3 large eggs, beaten
1 ½ C AP flour
3 t. baking powder
Salt & pepper
Olive oil and butter for cooking

Break salmon up into large mixing bowl. Add eggs and mix well. Add flour and mix well. In a separate bowl, add baking powder to salmon liquid; beat with whisk until foamy. Add to salmon mixture; add salt and pepper and mix well.

Heat olive oil and butter (start with about ½ C each) to a large cast-iron skillet; heat until very hot but not smoking. Put salmon, one large tablespoon at a time, in the hot oil. Flatten croquettes slightly so they'll cook evenly. Turn when done on one side (should be about two minutes per side). Put croquettes on serving tray lined with paper towels. Keep croquettes warm on a rack in the oven until all are cooked and you are ready to serve.

CRISPY OVEN-FRIED FISH
We have been cooking this, or a version of this, for decades, since it seemed for a time everyone was dieting and avoiding fried foods. But although this is low-fat, the crispiness of the fish will certainly "hook" your taste-buds!

    1 lb delicate-flavored white fish
    LIQUID MIXTURE
    ¼ C buttermilk
    1 T Dijon mustard
    Mix both together and let sit for about 15 minutes to let the flavors mingle.
BREADING
    ½ C cornmeal OR Panko breadcrumbs
    1 t each salt, onion powder, garlic powder, dill and paprika
    ½ t each pepper, thyme and cayenne pepper

Lemons for garnish

Place a cooling rack over a cookie sheet lined with aluminum foil. Turn oven on "Low Broil." Mix cornmeal and seasonings together; pour into a pie-pan or paper plate for easy dredging. Dredge each piece of fish first in the buttermilk mixture, then in the breading mixture. Gently place on the rack. When you've finished all the filets this way, put rack-cookie sheet in oven; broil for about 4 minutes, turning each filet gently. Serve with lemon wedges.

CHAPTER 9

GRAINS, LEGUMES & PASTA

This is one of Jeanne Franklin Lacey's (Eric's Mom's) recipes. This one is of narrative style—she just told it to me instead of writing it down—and I decided to keep it that way.

BAKED MACARONI & CHEESE

Prepare 12 oz pkg macaroni, rinse in cold water (note: I myself rinse it in hot water); set aside in colander. Butter a 2 qt casserole dish and set aside. Melt ½ stick of butter in saucepan. Stir in 4 T AP flour until smooth. Blend in 1 ½ C milk, 1 ½ t salt, ¼ t pepper. Stir until sauce thickens; keep stirring as the sauce may stick to bottom of saucepan before you know it. Add 6 oz. sliced sharp cheddar cheese and stir until melted. Combine with cooked macaroni in casserole. Sprinkle top with buttered breadcrumbs and parmesan cheese. Dot top with butter and bake in a 350° oven for 20 minutes. Serve immediately.

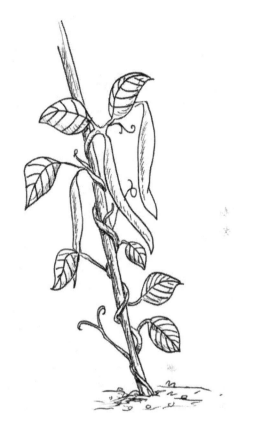

GREEK STYLE SHRIMP LOW-CARB PASTA SALAD

Eric made this up the night of March 3, 2020—the election primaries. We had it hot the first night but, served cold, is a delicious and flavorful pasta salad.

    1 pound, IQF shrimp, headed and peeled
    2 cloves fresh garlic, peeled and minced
    GREEK SALAD
    Feta, chopped
    Green olives, chopped and pitted
    Kalamata olives, same
    Cherry tomatoes, halved
    Bell pepper, finely chopped
    Half a cucumber, peeled and finely chopped
    Cavender's Greek seasoning to taste
    Olive oil

Balsamic vinegar
Butter

Make a Greek salad with the veggies and feta and put it in a bowl. Add olive oil, Greek seasoning and balsamic and mix well (but gently).
In a skillet, heat olive oil and a tablespoon of butter. Add minced garlic and shrimp. Lightly saute shrimp with a bit of Cavender's.

Let shrimp cool then combine with the salad and toss. Serve over a bed of lukewarm pasta (Dreamfield's is the best low-carb).

PREPARING CREAMER PEAS AND ALMOST ALL FRESH OR FROZEN PEAS, BEANS AND SQUASH

Creamers don't freeze well—you must get them fresh. They're expensive when you buy them at the produce market, but well worth it.

Eric perfected this dish on August 15, 2020. After schools here closed March 17, 2020, due to the China virus, the students were finally back to school this week. While writing down this recipe, I was also grading papers in the kitchen, washing hands frequently while doing so, as the pandemic was still ongoing.

1 pound creamer peas—fresh

½ Vidalia onion, chopped
1 T. bacon grease
1 T chicken stock (from jar concentrated bouillon is quick and fine)

In a 2 qt. saucepan, put bacon fat and onions in and saute until onions are translucent. Start a kettle of 3 quarts water to boil while sautéing onions. When onions are translucent, add peas. Stir and saute peas and onions for about 3-4 minutes.

Add chicken stock; add enough boiling water to the peas to cover, plus about ¼ inch. Stir together carefully; simmer at low for at least one hour. Stir occasionally, gently. After an hour, stir gently and see if they need to cook longer. If they're at all firm, keep cooking--they need to be soft.

When cooked perfectly, serve in ramekins with whatever seasoning you want.

You can do this with white beans, butter beans, and anything other than Great Northerns! Eric says "Great Northerns will fall apart if you cook 'em like this."

AUNT JOANN BAGWELL'S BLACK-EYED PEAS
(From Theresa)
Aunt Joann was visiting my Aunt Juanita in 2013. She cooked this with "Aunt 'Nee" and me. I was amazed at how much better this version tasted, as opposed to canned peas!

1 lb. bag dry peas
2 T. dry onion soup mix
2 t. chili powder
1 t. salt
¼ t. black pepper
1 large jalapeno pepper, seeded and diced
1 smoked ham hock
5 C water

Pick through the peas, discarding anything you don't want (like tiny stones). Rinse peas. Fill large pot with water and cover peas 2 inches above the top of the peas. Soak overnight, covered, at room temperature.

Next morning, drain and rinse peas. Add 5 cups water to the pot along with all other ingredients. Bring to boil and turn down the burner to where it's on simmer. Simmer, stirring occasionally, for one hour. Best served hot with corn pones.

OLD-FASHIONED BAKED BEANS
(From Theresa)
My grandmother, Simmie Catherine Parker Bagwell, wouldn't even give a second glance at canned baked beans. She also never wrote down a recipe, but a few times she let me in her

kitchen to watch how she cooked. This recipe is one she'd been making since the early 1900's. This particular recipe serves about 12 people.

10 C water
2 C dried pinto beans (about 1 pound)
½ C brown sugar packed
¼ C molasses
Dash salt
6 slices thick-sliced bacon, cooked to crispness and crumbled
1 medium onion, chopped
3 C water

In a deep pot (I use a Dutch oven), heat 10 C water and beans to boiling. Boil, uncovered, 3 minutes. Stir in remaining ingredients except for the 3 C water. Cover; bake at 350 for 4 hours, stirring every now and then. After 4 hours, remove pot from oven; stir in the 3 C water. Remove lid and bake, uncovered, for about 2 to 2 ½ hours more, stirring occasionally.

CHAPTER 10

MEAT & POULTRY DISHES

THERESA'S SWEET N' SOUR MEATLOAF
I created this recipe when Hurricane Elena struck Coastal Alabama in the mid-80s. We lived in Florence then (newlyweds), and we were preparing supplies and food to take down South and help in the clean-up effort. I wanted to make something to bring our family down in South Alabama that would taste even better the next day (or the next!), even if it was eaten cold or heated over a gas camp-stove, since no one had electricity.

    2 pounds ground chuck*
    1 large onion, chopped fine
    black pepper—as much as you like
    24 individual saltines, crushed **
    1 C tomato sauce
    2 eggs, sighty beaten

Mix together the meat and the onion in a large bowl. In another bowl, mix the pepper, tomato sauce and egg with saltines until the saltines are soft. Combine tomato mixture with meat and onion mixture until it's uniform. Shape into loaf in a greased loaf pan.

Pour this mixture over:
SAUCE
    4 T. apple cider vinegar
    ½ t. (or more) dry mustard
    4 T. brown sugar
    1 C tomato sauce
    ¼ C water (if you like your sauce thin)

Bake @ 350 degrees for one hour.

SUGGESTIONS:
*You can use ground venison, but it's so lean I add an extra egg so everything "sticks" together better.

**Instead of saltines, which is what I used to use, I have used Wheat-Thins and, for this particular loaf, regular oatmeal or Grape Nuts (allowing extra time for the egg/tomato sauce to soften the cereal before blending with the meat). If you use any kind of cereal, I recommend using about 1 cupful (some cereals I have used with success include all kinds of bran).

+ I have had terrible luck using ground turkey and ground chicken with this recipe.

MAMA'S MEATLOAF
This recipe is one of my mom's favorites.

> 3 pounds lean ground beef
> ½ pounds mild or hot Jimmy Dean Sausage
> 2 eggs, beaten
> ½ C bell pepper, chopped
> 1 C Vidalia onion, chopped
> 1 C mashed, cooked vegetables (she recommends carrots or one C. mixed veggies, mashed)
> Garlic, salt and pepper to taste
> 3 C old-fashioned oatmeal
> Dash each ketchup, Worcestershire sauce and mustard

In a large bowl, mix all the above ingredients well; form into two small or one large loaf pans (sprayed with non-stick).

Pour over loaves/loaf this sauce:
> 1 small can tomato sauce
> ¼ C brown sugar (or monk-fruit sweetener)

Mix sauce and sugar well together, pour over meatloaf, and bake at 350 degrees for about an hour or until sauce is bubbly. Note: two small loaves might bake in about ¾ time of one large loaf. This particular recipe will serve about 8 adults or two starving teenage boys.

ITALIAN STUFFED FLANK STEAKS
Our dear friend, Debbie Swindell Flynt, shared this recipe with me decades ago. The first time I made it, I knew it was a winner!

> 1 large flank steak
> 2 T Parmesan cheese
> 6 slices uncooked bacon
> 4 slices Provolone or Monterey Jack cheese

64

7 slices salami
1 small sweet onion, sliced thinly
1 can tomato sauce (14 oz)
Italian herbs
Garlic powder to taste
Optional: one layer of fresh, washed, drained and chopped spinach

Butterfly the steak. Do not cut all the way through. Place between 2 sheets of plastic wrap. Pound with mallet until the steak is of uniform thickness. Remove top plastic; sprinkle meat with Parmesan cheese. Place bacon strips across steak. Make layers of Provolone cheese, onions and salami. Lift plastic wrap and use it to help start making roll as tight as possible. Using baker's twine, tie rolled-up meat with string one inch apart lengthwise. Brown roll in hot oil; cover with Italian gravy (tomato sauce, herbs, garlic, and onions) and bring to a boil then cover and simmer for 3 hours, basting occasionally. Skim off fat. Slice and serve with gravy. This recipe serves 6-8.

CHICKEN WINGS
This is another of our friend Deb Flynt's favorites.

15 chicken wings (drumettes and flats)

Combine ½ C soy sauce, 1/4 C sugar, 1 t minced fresh ginger, 10 drops tabasco, ½ C water, 2 cloves garlic, minced, 2 T lemon juice and 2 T honey. Pour over wings and bake at 350 for 1 ½ hours. Turn and baste while cooking.

POLLO VALENCIA
(From Theresa)
I first tried this dish in the summer of 2010 at a trendy restaurant in Valencia, Spain, overlooking the lovely Port of Valencia, which is where the Turia River meets the Mediterranean Sea. Maybe it was the fresh, salty air or the ambience of the place, but I raved so much about this dish that, once home, I had to try and recreate it myself. Note to readers: don't be put off by the addition of white (golden) raisins. Instead of tasting "fruity," this chicken dish becomes surprisingly savory with the addition of the white raisins. This dish is also amazingly easy: the most time-consuming thing is sauteing the chicken thighs (the rest is a breeze).

3 pounds chicken thighs (cooking time is for bone-in)
3 T butter, unsalted
½ C onion, chopped 1 medium clove garlic, minced
1 8-oz can tomato sauce (I use salt-free)
¾ C chicken broth
2 T Apple Cider Vinegar
¼ t chili powder
½ C light (white) raisins
½ C pimiento-stuffed green olives, sliced

1 bell pepper, cut into strips

In a cast-iron skillet, brown chicken in butter; set aside chicken. Add onion and garlic to skillet; saute until lightly browned. Add remaining ingredients to skillet except bell pepper. Return chicken to skillet; spoon sauce and veggies over chicken. Cover and simmer 30-45 minutes. Add bell pepper and simmer about 15 minutes more. Serve over rice. As prepared, this dish serves 6 regular people or two teenage boys.

EASY SKINNY CHICKEN
(From Theresa)
This dish is one I came up with when on a rigorous diet. Although it's low in fat and calories, your guests will never know it—it's that delicious. An added plus is that it only takes about a half-hour to make!

    1 lemon
    4 slices ginger, each about a quarter sized
    4 t olive oil
    4 skinless, boneless chicken breasts or thighs (totaling 1 pound)
    1 T cornstarch
    ½ C chicken broth, low sodium
    3 cloves garlic, finely chopped
    1 C fresh scallions, cut into 2-inch lengths
    ½ t sugar or monk fruit sweetener
    ¼ t red pepper flakes
    ¼ t freshly ground black pepper
    Dash salt

Grate the zest from half the lemon. Cut the rest of the lemon into paper-thin slices. Mince the ginger. In a heavy skillet and over medium-high heat, heat 2 teaspoons of the olive oil until hot. Add chicken; saute about 3 minutes on each side until golden brown. Remove chicken and cover loosely.

In a bowl, dissolve the cornstarch in chicken broth. Add the other 2 teaspoons of olive oil to the skillet. When it's hot, add lemon zest, ginger, garlic and scallions. Cook, stirring constantly, for a couple of minutes.

Add the cornstarch-chicken broth mixture to the skillet; bring to a boil, stirring constantly. Add the chicken back to the skillet. Add the lemon slices, pepper flakes, sugar, and black pepper; return to a boil, then cover, and turn heat to simmer. Simmer until the chicken is cooked through, about 20-30 minutes, or until your meat thermometer registers 160 degrees. If desired, add dash salt and serve "as is" or over rice, low-carb pasta or riced cauliflower.

PIG PIE

Eric made this up when we were watching the Summer Olympics of 2020. They were held in Tokyo and it was actually the summer of 2021 (but they called it 2020 due to the Olympics being canceled because of the China virus). We had this with creamer peas (see that recipe in Chapter 9, Grains, Pasta & Legumes).

1 ½ lb ground pork
½ Vidalia onion
½ red bell pepper, chopped
Handful of basil, oregano, and sprig of fresh sage, all chopped
Dusting of onion and garlic powder
2 eggs, beaten
3 C shredded sharp cheddar cheese, divided
½ C sour cream
1 pie crust, lightly baked

Brown pork and drain. Save grease. After pork cools, add cheese and sour cream. Saute herbs and chopped veggies in reserved grease, and garlic and onion powders and mix well. Taste and add kosher salt if needed. After mixture has cooled, add beaten eggs and mix well.

Bake crust in cast-iron skillet until lightly brown. Fold mixture into pie crust and put remainder of cheese on top. Put in oven for 350 for about 16 minutes, then broil on low for 5-10 min until brown. Let sit about 10 minutes and serve hot.

PORK CHOPS DELLE VENEZIE

This was a great idea for a dish we created in spring of 2022 as a base for a phenomenal pork chop. This is unlike any pork chop you've ever had, anywhere.

2 pork chops, center cut, ¼ to ½ inch thick, deboned with the loin and filet sides separated and trimmed of excess fat, pounded on both sides to ½ of their original thickness
2 eggs, beaten
1 ½ C panko or 50-50 panko and breadcrumbs
pepper, garlic powder,
4 T *each* olive and Wesson oils
1 ½ C white vinegar

With meat cleaver, pound filets, sprinkle with pepper and garlic powder to your preference. Dredge both sides of chops in the egg wash, then coat in mixture of breadcrumbs and panko.

Heat in a skillet approx. 4 T each olive oil and Wesson oil in a cast iron skillet. In a separate skillet (nonstick or stainless), heat 1 ½ C white vinegar to a rolling boil. Fry pork chops in oil on both sides until golden brown. Put pork chops into the vinegar for approx. 3 min per side. Set pork chops in a glass dish in the oven at 350 for about 4-10 minutes as you warm dinner plates. From here, you can make a separate picatta sauce or a delicate chanterelle and butter sauce, or just serve as the venerated fried pork chop. The vinegar makes it super tender and gives it its own salty twang.

This pairs well with a dry white wine, or a sparkling wine such as Prosecco.

SAVORY BAKED CHICKEN

This is a "never-fail," "standby" recipe, but we've only had luck with this using Springer Farms chicken. Those other "baking hens" can turn out rubbery. We've had them literally impossible to pull the legs off after baking.

> 1 small (2+ pound) Springer Farms whole chicken
> Salt, pepper, garlic powder, Italian seasoning
> Fresh basil, oregano, rosemary and sage whole stems
> 2-3 T. olive oil (add more as needed)

In a cast iron skillet, coat chicken with olive oil. Season chicken with kosher salt, pepper, garlic and Italian seasoning, inside and out. Flip over, turning breast side up. Fill cavity with herbs. Tie legs and wings. Bake at 350 for 1 hour (meat thermometer should register 160 degrees).

Turn oven off, leaving chicken in until it reaches meat thermometer reading of 165 degrees. Remove from oven, let rest for about 10 minutes, and carve. Serve hot.

SAVORY CHICKEN WITH BROCCOLI

> 1 whole chicken, boiled, drained, & boned
> 1 C mayo
> 2 cans Cream of Chicken Soup
> 2 packages chopped, frozen broccoli, steamed
> ½ package Panko, seasoned
> ¾ t. curry powder
> Splash lemon juice
> 1 C butter, melted

In a casserole dish, combine first three ingredients. Place steamed broccoli on top. Cover with the Panko; add curry powder and lemon juice. Pour melted butter over. Bake at 350 degrees 30 minutes or until Panko is golden brown. Remove from oven and serve immediately.

CARNITAS (PRESSURE COOKER VERSION)

These are basically corn "street tacos" with what Eric had left over from a pork butt he'd cooked in a multi-pot (electric pressure cooker). He deboned and cubed a 6-lb Boston butt, leaving all the fat.

> 6 lb Boston Butt
> To taste: 1 t salt

1 T cumin
1 T smoked paprika
1 T garlic powder
1 T dried oregano
2 six-inch sprigs rosemary, washed and diced
3 cloves fresh garlic, peeled, "smashed," and chopped
1 T Wesson veg. oil
¼ C chicken bouillon
1 T Apple Cider Vinegar

Cut pork butt into 2" cubes. Roll in spice mix. Set aside. Heat oil in electric pressure cooker on "sear" setting and brown each piece of pork, turning frequently, and setting seared pieces aside. Deglaze with the chicken bouillon and vinegar solution, adding back the seared pork and set pressure cooker on "meat" and the time for 50 minutes.

When cooking cycle ends, release steam and separate what you can of the fat from the meat, retaining the meat in the liquid. This is "carnitas." It can be cooled, stored, frozen and reused for tacos, enchiladas and just about anything you would want to use pulled pork for.

PULLED PORK PIZZA PIE

Eric made up this dish when Mom was visiting in June of 2021. We had a pie crust instead of a pizza crust and he thought "Why not?" It was an instant hit!

1 pie crust, baked
3 C pulled pork, using recipe for Carnitas, above
½ Vidalia onion, diced
½ bell pepper, chopped
3 large cloves garlic, crushed
One handful each fresh basil and oregano leaves, cleaned and stemmed and coarsely chopped
1 C pitted whole Kalamata olives
20 or so cherry tomatoes, halved
1 egg, slightly beaten
1 C each Parmesan and sharp cheddar cheese
1 ½ C marinara sauce (we used Allessi) chunky
Dash white wine

Preheat oven to 400 degrees. Place pie crust in lightly greased cast-iron skillet until baked. Coat pie crust shell with the cheddar cheese, put pulled pork on top. Meanwhile, saute until translucent the onion, bell pepper and garlic.

Add marinara sauce and a dash of white wine. Bring to a boil, stirring constantly. Remove from heat and let cool.

Add olives and tomatoes and herbs to the sauce as it cools. Add beaten egg to sauce after it's cooled. Add ½ the parmesan cheese and whip well.

Cover top of pie with this mixture. Top with remaining Parmesan cheese.

Bake at 350 for 30 min. until firm then turn broiler on to brown the cheese. Let sit for about 10 minutes and serve.

SPANISH-STYLE CHEESY CHICKEN
Eric made this the night of June 27, 2021. It was a bit of an experiment but turned out "muy bien"!

    4 chicken thighs, skinned
    ½ can Rotel tomatoes, drained
    1 can green enchilada sauce, mild
    1 jalapeno, chopped
    ¼ Vidalia onion, chopped
    2 large cloves garlic, smashed and diced
    Dash each cumin and Adobo seasoning
    ½ C shredded Mexican cheese

Put the chicken thighs in the enchilada sauce to marinate for at least 1 hour, better overnight. In a skillet, brown chicken thighs in a bit of bacon fat or olive oil. After sufficient time, remove chicken thighs, and brown jalapeno, onion and garlic adding a little olive oil or 1 T. bacon fat until soft. Add enchilada sauce/marinade onto the sautéed veggies. Add the ½ can of Ro-Tel then add back and cover thighs in combined ingredients. Dust top with a little cumin and Adobo; bake at 350 for 45 minutes. Put shredded Taco-blend cheese on top and pop back in the oven until bubbly and cheese is melted, roughly 15 minutes. Serve with Mexican rice.

HURRICANE SALLY STEAK AU POIVRE
We made this the second night after getting power restored after Hurricane Sally, 9-19-2020. Eric bought two filet mignons and we had them with baked sweet potatoes and canned asparagus (we couldn't find fresh asparagus because the grocers were still getting in produce).
Note: MUST HAVE a sous vide!

2 filet mignons
Marinade: ¼ C Dale's
2 large cloves garlic, smashed and minced
Mrs. Dash (they changed the name to Dash, but in our book it's still Mrs. Dash)
3 T unsalted butter
2 T each unsalted butter and Bleu cheese
¼ C dry red wine

Put Dales and garlic into a quart zip-loc bag. Add filets. Let filets come to room temp while preparing sous vide, set to 120 degrees.

When sous vide is ready, immerse filets and cook in sous vide for one hour. About 10 min before removing steaks from SV, in a cast iron skillet on high heat, bring 3 T unsalted butter to a point where it's melted and just starting to smoke. Take filets out of SV; put on a plate. Dust each surface with Mrs. Dash, and pan-sear both sides of filet in the butter.

Meanwhile, melt 2 T unsalted butter and 2 T bleu cheese in a cup in the microwave. Sear both sides of filets until well seared over high heat. Reduce heat, remove filets to heated plates. Add butter/bleu cheese mix and ¼ C red wine to deglaze. Stir together, pour over filets and serve immediately.

LAURA JONES' THANKSGIVING SPECIAL BROWN SUGAR BOURBON HAM
My daughter Sarah Lacey Jones' mother-in-law Laura made this for us Thanksgiving of 2020. She was kind enough to share her recipe with me.

1 (7 lb) fully cooked ham half
2 C brown sugar, firmly packed, divided (into separate cups)
2 T Dijon mustard
2 cans beer
2 T honey
½ C bourbon

Place ham, fat side up, in a deep roasting pan. Press 1 cup of the sugar into all sides of the ham. Pour beer into pan. Insert meat thermometer, making sure it doesn't touch bone or fat. Cover and bake at 350 degrees for 30 minutes.

Remove 2 cups of the drippings from the roasting pan. Combine these drippings in a saucepan with the rest of the brown sugar, honey, mustard, and bourbon. Cook over medium heat, stirring constantly, until sugar dissolves. Baste ham with this mixture and return ham to oven.

Bake uncovered for 1 hour, basting every 10 minutes with sugar-bourbon mixture, until thermometer registers 140 degrees. Remove from oven and let rest 10 minutes before slicing.

This yields about 14 servings.

ROAST PORK LOIN WITH THYME & GARLIC
This is a recipe my sister-in-law, Cindy Barnett Lacey, shared with me. Everything that comes from her kitchen is wonderful, and this dish is no exception.

    3 T fresh thyme, chopped
    3 T extra virgin olive oil
    4 large cloves garlic, peeled and minced
    2 T lemon juice
    ½ t lemon zest
    1 center-cut boneless pork loin, 3-4 lbs
    pepper & salt (preferably kosher) to taste
    handful of Bay leaves and sprigs of thyme for garnish

Preheat the oven to 425 degrees. In a small bowl, combine thyme, olive oil, garlic, lemon juice and zest. Rub this mixture over all sides of the pork. Put pork, fat side up, on roasting rack in a roasting pan. Sprinkle lightly with kosher salt and pepper (diners can always add more).

Roast for 10 minutes; reduce oven temperature to 350; continue roasting an additional 50-60 minutes longer or until meat thermometer reads 160 degrees. Remove roast from oven; let rest about 5 minutes before slicing and serving. This particular recipe serves 6-8.

NANA'S CHICKEN & DUMPLINGS

My kids, Sarah and Gus, call my Mom "Nana." Every time she would visit, the kids begged her to make two things: biscuits and gravy (see chapters on Breads and Sauces, respectively) and this recipe. Her mother, my grandmother Simmie Catherine Parker Bagwell, brought this recipe from Texas to her home in north Alabama when she married and moved to my grandfather Leo Bagwell's farm. So this has been in the family for at least four generations.

> 6-7 chicken thighs
> Water to cover chicken and make broth—about a quart
> Dash salt
> ½ stick butter, melted
> 2 C SR flour
> 2/3 C COLD water
> 1 quart chicken broth
> ½ stick butter
> 1 t black pepper
> 2 t sage
> 1-2 stalks celery, diced fine and sautéed

In large pot, place chicken thighs; cover with water and dash of salt; cover and boil 'til tender. Remove thighs from pot to cool. Save broth in pot to boil dumplings.

When thighs are cool enough to handle, remove skin, bones, and any unwanted meat/fat. Cut meat into bite-size pieces and set aside (do not add back to pot until later).

DUMPLINGS

Put SR flour in a bowl and make a "well" in the center. Add melted butter and blend. Add the cold water and mix with a fork (or hands) to make a stiff dough. On floured dough-board, gently knead dough until very stiff dough ball is formed (it's important that your dough is stiff).

Move pot to back of stove. Add another quart of broth and heat back up. Add the ½ stick butter, pepper, sage and celery. With sharp knife or pizza cutter, cut dough into 2-inch pieces. Drop dough piece-by-piece into gently boiling seasoned broth, until you have used all the dough. Stir gently with wooden spoon to keep dough from sticking together and cook 5-10 minutes.

Add chicken pieces back to the pot; cover and simmer 15 minutes. Best served hot. Leftovers freeze well. This will serve 8-10 people.

TIM DOLAN'S TRI-TIP GRILLED ROAST BEEF
Our friend originally from Maine, Tim Dolan is an excellent chef, and for some years was our next-door neighbor in Fairhope. He was so excited about the way his beef turned out the first time he made this, he brought us some while it was still hot. This cut comes from the bottom of the sirloin, but cooked this way it is very tender, juicy and tasty.

1 tri-tip cut of beef, 2 ½ pounds
2 t each salt, onion powder, dried rosemary, garlic powder and black pepper
1 ½ t paprika (we used smoked paprika when we made this for ourselves)
¼ t cayenne pepper
1/3 C each red wine vinegar and vegetable oil
4 cloves garlic, crushed
½ t Dijon mustard

Stir seasonings together in a bowl. Place beef in a glass baking dish and coat it on all sides with the seasoning mixture. Cover with plastic wrap and refrigerate for at least 4 hours. We prefer to marinade it overnight in a Ziploc bag, air removed.

After marinating, take beef from refrigerator; uncover and allow to sit at room temperature for at least a half-hour. Meanwhile, combine vinegar, oil, crushed garlic and Dijon mustard in a sealable container; cover and shake to blend ingredients.

Prepare outdoor grill to cook the beef at a high-heat setting.

When beef has come to room temp, place it on the prepared grill; brush with garlic and vinegar mixture. Cook meat for 5 minutes, then turn and baste again. Repeat this on all sides until beef starts to look dark on the outside, about 30 minutes total. Your thermometer should read 130 degrees when the beef is ready. Remove from grill, let rest 10 minutes, then slice *across the grain* - very important - and serve, using any leftover basting sauce if desired.

Eric cooks the tri-tip "low and slow" in the Green Egg - set up for smoking (see "Cooking Methods" in Chapter 1), basting every 15 minutes after 1 ½ hour of smoking until 130 degrees is reached. Remove, wrap in foil and let rest before slicing across the grain.

HAM & CHEESE ROLLS
(From Theresa)
My Aunt Joye Bernice Collins gave me this recipe. She made these for holiday gatherings, family reunions, and picnics on the ground (on cemetery-decorating days).

1 stick butter
1 T brown sugar
1 T Worcestershire Sauce
2 T yellow mustard
1 T poppy seed
1 pkg. crescent rolls

    1 lb sliced ham lunch meat
    1 lb sliced "American" cheese

On stovetop or in microwave, melt first five ingredients and mix well. On a dough board, roll out each crescent roll. Brush or spread each with a little more melted butter. Inside each roll, layer with slices of cheese and cooked, sliced ham. Roll up and place rolls on a greased cookie sheet. Spoon the 5-ingredient mixture over each roll. Bake at 350 degrees about 20 minutes until golden brown.

THAI STYLE GROUND PORK AND VEGGIES

We created this April 28, 2020. States were declaring a re-opening of businesses as we watched an end to the lockdown on the evening news. We would learn later that this was not going to happen—not until spring of 2021.

    2 lbs ground pork
    1 C shredded cabbage
    1 zucchini peeled, quartered and sliced
    2 C mushrooms, sliced
    4 shallots, sliced
    3 chili peppers, sliced thinly
    4 large cloves garlic, diced
    SAUCE
    1 T rice wine vinegar
    1 T each soy sauce and fish sauce
    1 t chopped garlic
    1 t sliced chili peppers (OK to substitute Jalapeno if no chili peppers available)
    2 T sliced fresh ginger

Chop the veggies and set aside. In a saucepan, cook pork until done - "pebbled" is what Eric calls it - break up all the big hunks into the smallest granular size possible using a spoon. Drain but reserve stock. Take about ½ cup of pork juice and saute remaining diced garlic, ginger and chili peppers until brown. Add and saute veggies in oil; add some of the reserved pork fat if needed.

Combine pork with veggies and garnish with the herbs. Use soy sauce and fish sauce to taste. Serve over rice.

COCONUT CURRIED PORK TENDERLOIN WITH VEGGIES & RICE
 We cooked this the night of May 4, 2020. The Alabama beaches had just reopened (closed due to the China coronavirus) and the weather had been spectacular, although Mobile Bay itself was still extremely muddy.

    1 pork tenderloin, about 2 pounds
    1 4 oz. can Thai green curry (Nam Prik Maesri) paste

1 15-oz can PLAIN coconut milk
1 each yellow and zucchini squash, washed and cubed
Thai basil double handful, washed and lightly chopped (leaves)
3 green onions, chopped
1 C fresh mushrooms, washed and sliced

Mix coconut milk and curry paste together; whisk with a wire whisk until smooth. Pour half over the pork in a cast iron skillet. "Paint" the pork with the milk-curry paste and let sit at room temperature 30 min. Chop the squashes, mushroom and green onion. Put in a large stock pot with a fitted lid. Add the other half of the curry-coconut milk mixture. Heat on low until bubbling, stirring frequently. Turn off and leave covered.

Pre-heat oven to 375. Place pork in cast iron skillet in center of oven rack and bake approx. 30 min. until it reaches 140 degrees (meat thermometer). Remove from oven; let sit 10 minutes. Return veggie mixture to a low boil. After 10 min., dice pork into large bite-size chunks and add to all drippings and veggies. Stir thoroughly and cover. Let return to a bubble, then turn off. Serve over hot jasmine rice with the fresh Thai basil for garnish.

THAI-STYLE CRUNCHY CHICKEN FINGERS WITH SAUTEED BOK CHOY, HERBS AND VEGETABLES
This zero-carb dinner we created on June 15, 2020.

1 lb boneless, skinless chicken fingers
½ C SR flour
½ C corn starch
1 T salt
1 t smoked paprika
1 t lime powder
Handful each of fresh Thai basil, fresh oregano, two sprigs mint
1 stalk fresh lemongrass
3 large cloves garlic, peeled, smashed and chopped

½ C chopped red, yellow, orange bell peppers
1 T+ sriracha chili garlic sauce
2 baby bok choy, chopped

Combine dry ingredients, whipped together thoroughly; add water to desired consistency. Preheat a deep-fat fryer, filled with enough peanut oil to fry the chicken, to 350 degrees. Coat chicken fingers in dry ingredients-water mixture. Fry until golden brown, then place on rack in warm oven. Meanwhile, in a wok, heat a T. sesame oil and 1 T. olive oil until hot. Put in bok choy and all herbs and vegetables. Stir-fry until lightly coated and slightly wilted, about 3 minutes.

Remove from heat and cover. Make a sauce with the T. soy sauce, 1 t. sesame oil, and 1 T. sriracha; blend well (add lime juice, more to taste).

Serve the chicken on a mound of veg/herbs with the sauce and a spoon.
This is as good as a similar dish we've had at a restaurant in Bangkok. Our Thai friend Opas loved this when we cooked it for him while visiting us!

LOWER ALABAMA-STYLE FRICASSEE POULET
This dish has its origins in France, but Southerners have adapted it and made more than one version of this. One simple recipe calls for roasted chicken with a cream soup poured over it and served over rice. This particular adaptation of the classic French method is a little more labor-intensive, but when you taste it, you'll say, "Ooh la-la, y'all!"

4-6 chicken thighs
olive oil
1 can cream of mushroom (or mushroom and chicken) soup
Herbs Aux Provence
salt
pepper
garlic powder
2 C cooked white rice

Place about 2 T olive oil in a large iron skillet or glass baking dish. Roll thighs in oil ending with skin side down. Season with a dash of salt and pepper, garlic powder and herbs aux provence on both sides, ending with the skin side up.

Cook thighs for 45 minutes at 350 degrees. Remove from oven and remove thighs to another pan to hold while thoroughly mixing the cream of mushroom soup into the drippings. Add the cooked rice, mixing well. Replace thighs on top and place back in oven for 10-15 minutes or until it is bubbling. Serve hot.

ERIC LACEY'S CHICKEN FRIED VENISON STEAKS AND GRAVY
Eric first made this for our friends, Les and Carole King, February 2006. He had actually made it many times before over the course of several decades, but this night's dish was the best, so I wrote it down.

    1 large or 2 medium onions, diced
    2 beef bouillon cubes in 2 ½ C boiling water
    1 C Self-Rising flour
    ½ C Vegetable oil
    2-3 cloves garlic, minced
    Dash granulated garlic or garlic powder
    S&P
    4-6 cubed venison steaks - if not "cubed," use tenderloin, sliced ¼" and pounded well
    Dash red wine
    2-3 bay leaves
    4 C cooked white rice

Dust steaks on both sides with salt, pepper and garlic powder. Generously flour both sides. In Dutch oven, fry in hot oil, being careful not to let the oil or steaks burn. When browned on both sides, remove steaks; set aside. Put in onions and garlic; saute until onion is translucent. Deglaze with red wine. Put steaks back in Dutch oven; gently pour hot bouillon until it just covers steaks. Add bay leaves; cover and gently simmer for 1 hour or until you can't stand the delicious aroma anymore!

PRESENTATION:
Place steaks on a bed of freshly cooked rice. Good served with biscuits or homemade bread and a hearty red wine.
Note: This recipe is great with pork chops and beef minute steaks. For chicken breasts, quail and dove breasts, substitute chicken stock for beef bouillon and deglaze with white wine.

THERESA'S "TRASH OR DINNER?" RECIPE, CREATED 9-10-14
This night, when looking around in the fridge for things that were close to being spoiled (thus, trash), I found the items listed below, created them into a casserole, and it made 12 delicious servings. Gus ate THREE servings by himself that night! This freezes well, too.

YOU WILL NEED: *
    2 T EACH olive oil and butter
    One small can black, chopped olives
    ½-3/4 C French fried onions (or, ½ an onion, chopped)
    ½ C sliced, fresh mushrooms
    ½ C EACH red and green peppers, chopped
    Garlic, minced, to your taste (I used 2 tablespoons)
    1 can (10 oz.) diced tomatoes, undrained
    1 can (10 oz.) cooked chicken breast, undrained, finely chopped
    1 T EACH parsley, sage and black pepper

1-2 Bay leaves
1 pkg. (8-10 oz.) Parmesan cheese, finely shredded
1 pkg. (8-10 oz) Sharp Cheddar cheese, shredded
1 pkg. angel-hair pasta (I used Dreamfield's Low Carb—no one can tell the difference)

In a cast-iron skillet (my preference), melt olive and butter; combine and saute next ingredients EXCEPT for cheeses.

After all vegetables are cooked and bubbly, add Parmesan cheese and stir thoroughly. Let sit while you boil pasta, following package directions (I suggest you break the pasta into 2-3" lengths—it serves easier that way).

Drain pasta, then mix it thoroughly with the vegetable-seasonings-cheese mixture. Pour into 9 x 11 greased baking pan (I use a non-stick).

Preheat oven to 350; while waiting, sprinkle the Cheddar cheese on top of the casserole. Bake until the cheese is melted and dish is bubbling again.

*HINT: these vegetables are only what I had left in the fridge; you can pretty much use anything you can find that's about to go bad!

THAI-STYLE TACOS

1 lb ground chuck, cooked, drained, pebbled, reserve fat
¼ Vidalia onion, minced
¼ green bell pepper, diced
3 cloves garlic, smashed and diced
Romaine Lettuce leaves, stalks cut out
1 t Lime powder
1 T *each* Soy sauce and Fish sauce
½ C sour cream
1 full T sushi grade ginger, minced
1 T Rice powder
¼ C *each* Fresh Thai basil, oregano, and cilantro

Cook beef; drain, put 2 T. retained liquid back into pot. Saute garlic, peppers and onions in the drippings until onions are translucent. Add beef, lime powder, soy sauce, ginger and rice powder and saute for a few minutes.

Add fish sauce then just before serving, add herbs. Toss and leave lid on for 10-15 minutes. Serve this way: "frost" lettuce leaves with sour cream, top with meat mixture, serve with hot steamed rice.

PUERCO RANCHERO

Eric invented this the night of January 18, 2021. I had said that I was having a craving for enchiladas, and he came up with this. You can also use this recipe with chicken.

YOU NEED:
Cumin, sprinkle
1 t Salt
½ t Badia chili-lime seasoning
½ can (2 oz) San Marcos chipotle salsa
Garlic powder, to taste (good dusting)
2 heaping T canned chipotle salsa
2 heaping T *each* Sour cream and Salsa (tomato)
2 C Taco/Mexican blend shredded cheese
1 2-pound pork tenderloin

Butterfly the tenderloin and put all ingredients inside the cut. Spread them inside and let the meat come to room temperature. Use toothpicks to close tenderloin. Seal tightly with aluminum foil.

Bake for 35 minutes on 350 or until thermometer registers at 140 degrees. Let rest for 15 minutes; slice and serve with gravy (we had mashed turnips, but rice works well). The sauce is fantastic!

THAI-ONE-ON STIR-FRY CHICKEN

Eric made this one on one of our rare, truly-cold nights in January of 2021. It's good comfort food!

You will need
4 chicken thighs, boned and skinned (save the skin)
½ head of cabbage, chopped
1 jalapeno, sliced thinly
1 "thumb" ginger, peeled and slivered
2 large cloves garlic, chopped and smashed
½ Vidalia onion, chopped
3 spring onions, chopped
6-8 white mushroom caps, washed & chopped
1 zucchini, peeled, quartered & chopped
Rice wine vinegar, soy sauce, garlic powder, Thai chili garlic sauce and oyster sauce

Start rice cooking while you make the chicken. Add 2 T oil in wok. Brown diced chicken skins and garlic on med-high heat until crispy. Drain and reserve both the oil and chicken skins (separately).

Bring wok back to high heat. Dust chicken with garlic powder and soy sauce. Put chicken and fry until lightly brown. Remove and set aside.

Put all veggies into the wok; stir, reducing veggies a bit as they cook. Add two big dashes rice wine vinegar and a tablespoon (to taste) Thai chili garlic & ½ small jar (1 cup) oyster sauce. Stir again.

Add chicken back to wok and blend with veggies. Cook a few minutes until it comes to a bubble, then turn on low and put a lid on.

Let cook for about 10 minutes. Meanwhile, take crispy-fried chicken skins and garlic and mince. Serve veggie-chicken mixture from the wok over hot rice, garnish with garlic-skins mixture.

LAMB SHISH KEBABS

    2 lbs boneless lamb, cut into 1 ½" cubes (can use boneless leg of lamb, just removed silver skin)
    2 sweet red peppers, quartered
    2 green peppers, quartered
    1 jar whole boiled onions (or slice an onion in half and saute till half soft)
    1 C garlic flavored French dressing
    2 T red wine vinegar

Mix vinegar with French dressing in a deep bowl. Marinate the meat cubes and quartered peppers in the sauce overnight in refrigerator, or 3 hours at room temperature (covered). Fill skewers, alternating meat cubes with green and red peppers and onions. Broil until lamb is cooked medium well. Brush with the remaining marinade while turning frequently. Serve with steamed rice.

HERB-ENCRUSTED RACK OF LAMB ON THE GRILL
This lamb dish is deceptively easy—even folks who are a bit daunted at the thought of turning out a good rack of lamb say this has worked for them every time.If you are worried about the rib ends burning off in the grill, wrap rib ends in foil - though it is hard to keep the foil on while grilling - at least you tried.

    1 ½-2 lb rack of lamb, with fat trimmed away
    MARINADE
    3 cloves garlic, minced
    2 t *each* rosemary, oregano and mint (the latter optional for those who don't like mint)
    ½ lemon zest
    ½ t salt (we use kosher)
    ½ t pepper
    2 T olive oil

In a small bowl, combine all marinade ingredients (the mixture should be more like a paste). "Frost" the lamb with this mixture; wrap in plastic wrap and chill 6-8 hours, preferably overnight. Next morning, bring the lamb out of 'fridge and allow to come to room temperature (about a half-hour).

Set your grill on high (about 500 degrees). Watching the grill constantly to guard against flare-ups, place lamb fat side down. Sear meat for about 5 minutes.

Turn grill down to about 425 degrees. Turn lamb and roast for 14-15 more minutes. Internal temperature should read 120 degrees (for medium rare). Remove lamb from grill; place on cutting board and cover with foil to cook a bit more as it rests. After you see your thermometer register 125 degrees or so, cut the lamb into chops, place on serving platter and sprinkle with any additional herbs for presentation (maybe a few sprigs of fresh rosemary).

STUFFED BELL PEPPERS
Bell peppers are super easy to prepare, but there is one step that must be taken for maximum enjoyment: they *must* be blanched prior to stuffing and baking.

Makes 4 peppers:
1 lb ground beef chuck
1 lb ground "market" Italian sausage
½ chopped onion (yellow or vidalia)
2 cloves garlic, smashed, chopped
2 cans diced tomatoes
½ lb shredded cheese (Italian mix, cheddar, whatever you want)
4 large bell peppers (4 bumps on the bottom - best for standing upright), cored and white veins carefully removed

Core the peppers, removing seeds and white veins from inside. Place peppers in a large pot of boiling water and blanch them for 6-8 minutes. Remove carefully to colander and let drain/cool.

Brown beef and sausage together, blending, until pebbled. Remove from pan and drain fat, reserving 2 T in the pan.

Saute the onion and garlic until onion is clear; add diced tomatoes and meat mixture, stir until well blended.

Clear a spot for a pepper in skillet and fill with meat mixture, topping with cheese. Repeat until all 4 peppers are stuffed. Use remaining filling to keep peppers propped up.

Place in oven at 350 degrees for about 20 minutes, until meat bubbles and cheese is fully melted.

Goes great with rice!

POP'S SPAGHETTI SAUCE

Pop (Richard Cobb Lacey, Sr.) loved to spend a Sunday afternoon making spaghetti sauce. We all loved to spend Sunday evening eating it. There's nothing magical about it other than the memories. It took time, and always was accompanied by a "clumping" of family and friends. The cast of characters changed over time, and each occasion lives on in our minds through this recipe.

Serves: a bunch (10+?) Any leftovers freeze well.

2 lbs ground chuck
2 lbs market ground sausage
1 whole Vidalia onion, chopped
1 whole green bell pepper, cored, chopped and with white vein removed
6 cloves garlic, smashed and diced
2 handfuls of green olives, chopped
1 medium jar pimientos, sliced
2 cans diced tomatoes
1-2 cans tomato paste
2 cans tomato sauce
2 dashes Worcestershire sauce
4-5 bay leaves
1 T sage
2 T oregano
2 T basil
1 t black pepper
1 t sugar (this brings out the savoriness of the tomato sauce)
½ cup dry red wine (Chianti is best)
Maybe - maybe a little salt at the end.

Brown the chuck and the sausage in a big, deep pot (I use my Dutch oven), until pebbled. Add the diced tomatoes, tomato paste and tomato sauce. Bring to a very low simmer, stirring regularly. Add the spices and Worcestershire.

In a separate pan, saute the onion, bell pepper and garlic in a little olive oil until bell is softened and onion is translucent. Add the olives and pimientos. Bring to a bubble, add ½ cup good red wine (Chianti is best).

When bubble is restored, add sauteed veggies to meat and stir well to blend. Cover and let simmer on low for at least 1 hour.

Note: this sauce is best if it goes through a cool down - to warm then restored to serving temperature at simmer.

This is awesome as a pizza sauce, bread topper, zucchini filling, lasagna - anything that needs a red meat marinara sauce.

SHOMO BRAISED CABBAGE AND SAUSAGE SOUP
This is a dish that Eric perfected in his years of hunting at a friend's hunting camp, called Shomo. This feeds 4-6 hungry hunters--a hearty, hot meal without a lot of fuss or expense. A camp favorite!

    1 medium green cabbage, chopped, stem removed
    1 large Vidalia onion, chopped
    1 can diced tomatoes
    1 lb Conecuh sausage, chopped
    1 C boiling chicken stock
    2-3 T apple cider vinegar

In a deep pot or Dutch oven, fry the chopped Conecuh. When cooked, add cabbage and onions, stir to coat and saute for 10 or so minutes. Add the diced tomatoes and chicken stock; return to boil for 10 or so minutes, stirring frequently. Add apple cider vinegar at the end to taste.

PREPARING WILD GAME:
Many of the meat preparations in this section can be used with wild game. For best results, here are a few notable differences in the primary stage of wild game preparation.

Venison: Since there is so little fat in the meat there aren't a lot of options that will turn out moist and tender, every time.

If you are going to fry/saute some tenderloin medallions, cut the tenderloin into ½" pieces and pound with a meat hammer before sauteing quickly and eating on the rare side of doneness. This is excellent with butter-deglazed mushrooms and onions.

If it is a venison roast, your best chance at tenderness is in the pressure cooker. Make sure the roast is at least covered with beef bouillon. Don't cook for more than 30 minutes under pressure or it may get dry.

Venison shoulder is my favorite piece, rubbed with spices and smoked on the Big Green Egg. It has lots of bone, little meat, but it's always good. Slice it thin and serve with a balsamic reduction - or light BBQ sauce.

Pheasant is especially problematic. Breast meat is really the only part of the bird worth toiling with. Filet off the bone and beat the heck out of it. From there you can chicken fry it (see previous) or smother saute it - finished with a white wine/Dijon deglaze is nice. A good friend replied when asked if he wanted some pheasant we had shot: "Sure, I'll put them in the crab trap and trade up!" It's better eating than that, but expectations must be kept within certain bounds.

Dove is one of our favorites - we have 2 basic recipes: Chicken fried in gravy - which is really, really good (see earlier in this chapter) and the following:

GAME DAY SMOKED STUFFED DOVE BREASTS

> 12 dove breasts (still on the bone)
> 6 jalapenos
> ½ stick cream cheese, softened at room temperature
> 12 slices bacon
> toothpicks
>
> Marinade:
> 1 T sesame oil
> 2 T soy sauce
> 1 t garlic powder

Prepare marinade, place doves in a Ziploc bag; coat each breast, let sit at least 30 minutes (best overnight).

Remove caps from jalapenos, slice lengthwise, remove seeds, fill jalapeno halves with cream cheese.

Place dove breast cavity on top of stuffed jalapeno, wrap each in 1 piece of bacon, secure with a toothpick if needed.

Grill with soaked pecan chips on a low fire until brown - about 30 minutes. There are never any leftovers with this dish!

DUCK CARPACCIO
(From Eric)
Wild duck is another favorite of mine - and since I don't get it very often, I tend to prepare it this way - my favorite - especially with wood ducks or mallards.

> 4-6 breast filets (wood duck, mallard are best)
> 2 cloves garlic, minced
> Worcestershire sauce
> butter
>
> Marinade:
> 1 T sesame oil

2 T soy sauce
1 t garlic powder

Let marinade for at least 30 minutes.

In a skillet, combine 2 T butter, 1 t Worcestershire sauce and 2 cloves garlic, minced. Heat to medium high heat, place breast filets in pan, moving so they don't stick; cook 2-3 minutes each side. Remove from heat to cutting board. Slice (crosswise) about ¼"thick, then arrange on a heated plate. Heat to simmer the marinade and pour over slices. Serve immediately.

RABBIT
Rabbit is another critter we don't get that much of, but when we do we tend to chicken fry it after sectioning it up into front legs, back legs and loin. There are those who barbeque rabbit - and I admire them for it, however I usually have more people to feed than rabbits to cook, so some gravy and rice "spreads the good fortune."

There are other notable critters that abound in our Southern woods, but we're not chasing squirrels, snakes, opossums or racoons. Things just haven't gotten that hard - yet.

WILD BIRD POT PIE
(From Theresa)
My friend Rachel Swanson shared this recipe with me. We used pheasant for this recipe, and it was delightful.

2 pheasant breasts
4 C water
1 medium onion, cut into fourths
1 stalk celery, minced
2 T lemon juice
1 ¼ t salt
½ t pepper
¼ t Worcestershire sauce
⅛ t ground nutmeg
¾ C AP Flour
1 jar pearl onions, drained (optional)
1 pkg. frozen peas
½ C sliced carrots
1 small jar pimientos, drained
One pie crust

In Dutch oven, place bird breasts, water, onion, celery & garlic; bring to a boil. Reduce heat; cover and simmer one hour. Remove meat and let cool. When cool enough to handle meat, debone and set aside. Strain broth, saving vegetables to use as a side dish.

Measure 3 ½ C broth and put into saucepan. Add lemon juice, salt, pepper, Worcestershire sauce and nutmeg. Remove ½ C broth; stir flour in. Return to pan and bring to a boil. Boil 1 minute or until to desired thickness. Add onions, peas, carrots, pimientos and meat and mix well. Spoon into a baking dish. Shape pie crust to fit baking dish. Place pie crust over meat mixture and seal edges. Cut small vents in top of crust. Bake at 425 degrees for about 40 minutes or until crust is brown and inside is bubbling.

CHAPTER 11

SAUCES, DRESSINGS, SEASONING & CONDIMENTS

EASY, VERSATILE ROUX

Every good cook must have a good roux recipe in his or her culinary repertoire. In addition to gumbo, you can also make a roux as a base for gravies and to thicken soups.

  ¼ C bacon drippings
  1.4 C peanut oil
  ¼ C AP flour

Melt fat and oil in saucepan; whisk in flour gradually until smooth and there are no lumps. Let simmer for a minute or two (don't let it burn!); for a white/cheese sauce, let simmer an additional minute. For a dark roux (as in for a gumbo), stir and cook until it reaches a dark color. Add any liquid or seasonings you want at this point and use according to what you're cooking.

A good roux for gumbo will take about 1 hour of constant stirring and adding. Don't leave it for a minute - and don't get antsy and increase the temperature or it will burn in a second. If it burns, throw it out. It has no further purpose on this earth.

Eric gave up on making gumbo starting from a roux quite some time ago. He highly recommends Kary's jarred roux which can be added when you get your stock just like you want it, adding it in small increments without concern of having enough roux and being an hour out from having more.

WHITE SAUCE

Don't just add cheese to a dish - use this simple white sauce and do it right. This sauce takes the ordinary to the extraordinary if used on such dishes as macaroni and cheese, broccoli and cheese, cheesy squash casserole, etc.

> Melt ½ stick of butter in saucepan
> Stir in 4 T plain flour until smooth
> Blend in 1 ½ C milk, pepper to taste

Stir until sauce thickens, keep stirring as the sauce may stick to bottom of saucepan before you know it. Add more milk if too thick. Cook a bit longer, stirring constantly, if too thin.

Variations:
Substitute buttermilk for milk - you will need more than regular milk - but be mindful that the sauce will thicken quickly.
Add a bit of garlic powder, excellent in a cheese sauce over broccoli

See "HELENS CREAMY CHEESE SAUCE" below for additional riffs.

HOMEMADE AND VERSATILE SWEET & SOUR SAUCE
(From Theresa)
I originally made this in 1985 to go with "Theresa's Sweet 'n Sour Meatloaf." That entire recipe is in Chapter 10. You can use this sauce over all kinds of meats, such as chicken and pork.

> 4 T apple cider vinegar
> ½ t (or more) dry mustard
> 4 T brown sugar
> 1 C tomato sauce
> ¼ C water (if you like your sauce thin)

Mix all ingredients well and use it to bake, marinade, or for a sauce to pass around the table.

JON SWANSON'S ROAST MARINADE

Our friend Jon Swanson introduced us to this never-fail marinade when he and his wife Rachel had us over for dinner to taste the finished product back in the spring of 2021. We knew this one had to be in our cookbook!

½ C strong coffee
½ C soy sauce
1 T Worcestershire sauce
1 T ACV
1 T sesame seeds
2 T butter
1 large onion, finely chopped
meat tenderizer

Melt butter; add sesame seeds and all other ingredients. Dust roast on all sides with meat tenderizer. Pour marinade over roast; marinade 6-8 hours (better if done overnight).

ASIAN SAUCE

We use this in a variety of dishes such as fish and lamb dishes.

1 T rice wine vinegar
1 T each soy sauce and fish sauce
1 t chopped garlic
1 t sliced chili peppers
2 T sliced fresh ginger

In a skillet, saute garlic, chili peppers and fresh ginger until soft but not burned. Add rice wine vinegar, soy and fish sauces until the taste is to your liking. Pour over your fish/lamb and serve with hot cooked rice.

NO-FAIL, ALWAYS-PERFECT HOLLANDAISE SAUCE

(From Theresa)

When we were first married, and Eric was in Graduate School at The University of Alabama, we lived for a time in Tuscaloosa. We lived next door to a chef (Robert Greene) who worked at North Port Yacht Club. I'd go over to visit him and his wife, and after a while, he began to show me a few of his favorite recipes. This is one of the first I learned.

3 eggs separated (save the whites for meringue or an omelet)
1 stick very cold butter, halved
1 T lemon juice

Put the yolks into a saucepan and with a wooden spoon, stir very gently to break the yolks (Robert says, "A quick breaking will 'bruise' the yolks, and the flavor won't be as good.") With a butter cutter, take the first half-stick of the butter and run it through the cutter. Put the slices into the saucepan and turn heat on low (note to readers: if you just put the half-stick in without cutting it into slices, the eggs will tend to cook before the butter is all melted. With pieces of the cold butter being stirred around the eggs, you will have a better result).

With a whisk, stir constantly until the butter is melted. Immediately, add the other half-stick of butter, which you have also run through the butter-cutter. Cook, stirring constantly, until yolks are creamy and buttery. Stir in lemon juice. Turn off heat and let sit until you are ready to use the sauce for Eggs Benedict, fish, chicken, or some other dish.

Now, if you find you've cooked this sauce on too high a heat—OR if you got distracted and didn't stir it constantly—you may discover you've got what looks like buttery scrambled eggs. Here's how Robert said to fix that and turn the sauce creamy again: Whisk into the egg-butter mixture, one T. at a time, ICE WATER, until the sauce is of a creamy consistency.

HELEN'S CREAMY CHEESE SAUCE
Eric made this the night of May 24, 2021. He tasted it and said, "If Helen [of Troy) had made a cheese sauce that would, like her looks, launch a thousand ships, this would be it."

    3-4 cloves FRESH garlic, minced
    ½ stick unsalted butter
    1 C SR flour
    2 C whole buttermilk (not skim)
    1 T cracked pepper
    1 C white shredded cheddar
    ½ C shredded Velveeta

In a small saucepan, melt the butter. Lightly brown the garlic and cracked fresh black pepper, stirring constantly for approximately 5 minutes. Using a sieve, drain the butter from the garlic and reserve both.

Return liquid to the small pan. Slowly add approx. 2/3 cup SR flour, while stirring with a whisk. Slowly add (in ¼ cup increments), buttermilk, stirring constantly over low heat.

Keep whisking and adding buttermilk until you get the thinness or thickness you desire. Remove pan from heat and add approx. ½-3/4 cup cheddar and equal amount Velveeta. Add the reserved garlic and butter, whipping with a whisk.

That night, we had this sauce served over broccoli, and it was out of this world.

It can also be served with hearty bread as a dip. There have been incidents concerning the pan when finished - if you put the pan into the sink before allowing someone to "finger clean" it, you may face harsh (and well-deserved) criticism.

ASIAN-STYLE BARBECUE SAUCE AND MARINADE

We made this the night of May 19, 2021. You can make this sauce with so many types of proteins.

In a 12" skillet, under low heat, combine:
1 T bacon fat or olive oil
1 T sesame oil
3 T Korean Hoisin Sauce
Heat above on low until it bubbles. Once it bubbles, add
1 T rice wine vinegar
2-3 cloves fresh chopped garlic

Saute until sauce thickens, adding rice wine vinegar as needed. Remove from heat.

You can also use this with Italian dressing, but the key is to make the sauce in the pan, toss the protein in it, and bake.

Options: add curry, yogurt, pickled ginger

THAT'S AMORE! BALSAMIC ITALIAN DRESSING & MARINADE
(From Eric)
I've been making this for decades. It's one of those never-fail sauces or marinades. Meats turn out flavorful and tender, and it's excellent on salads.

1 T *each* Oregano, Marjoram, Thyme, Rosemary, Basil and Sage
1 Bay leaf, whole
¼ C *each* Balsamic and Apple Cider Vinegar (the latter with the "mother")

Mix all ingredients in a dressing carafe or jar with a tight-fitting lid. Refrigerate. If using as marinade, let sit in 'fridge for 1-2 hours before using on meat.

ERIC'S "DIRTY LITTLE SECRET" ITALIAN DRESSING AND MARINADE

The folks at Good Seasonings took the time and effort to make a perfect blend of spices and emulsifiers and created "Good Seasonings Italian Dressing."

Make it to recipe, using Wesson vegetable oil (not olive oil) in their carafe - EXCEPT - use a 50/50 ratio of balsamic vinegar and apple cider vinegar. I can't make it any better - and their stuff doesn't separate before I can get it out of the carafe.

BAM! ALMOST MAKES EMERIL LAGASSE JEALOUS REMOULADE DRESSING
(From Theresa)
One night around 2010 I was watching one of Emeril's cooking shows as we were making Oven-Fried Fish (see that recipe in Chapter 8). I thought to myself, "I can make a remoulade

sauce like his just with what I have here!" and this was the result. We served it for company to go with the fish and it was an instant hit.

> ½ C mayonnaise OR make a blend of mayo and Greek yogurt
> Dill, fresh, snipped, to taste
> S&P
> Lemon juice, splash
> 1 T *each* yellow mustard and ketchup
> 2 T dill relish (optional)
> Dill (for garnish)

Mix all ingredients together; adjust seasonings to your liking. Chill until ready to serve. Before putting serving bowl on table, top dressing with a little fresh snipped dill.

CARIBBEAN DREAM MANGO SALSA.
Created by the two of us cooking together one cold February night in 2014. We first used it to top baked fish.

> 1 fresh, diced mango
> Rice vinegar
> Sriracha sauce
> Dijon mustard
> Pepper

Mix mango w/all other ingredients to taste. Goes well with meats, on top of summer greens and even fried fish!

SHERRY'S BBQ SAUCE
This is my sister Mary's friend Sherry Havira. She shared it with me in October of 2009.

> 1 bottle Open Pit barbecue sauce
> ½ C ketchup, NO high fructose corn syrup
> ¾ t lemon juice
> ¼ C onion, minced
> Dash white wine
> Dash Crystal hot sauce

Combine all, heat to simmer then let cool.

ERIC'S QND TZATZIKI SAUCE
Wonderful sauce that can be served with lamb dishes, as a dip, or as an ingredient in Greek Coleslaw (see "FRUITS AND VEGETABLE DISHES")

> 1 ½ C plain Greek yogurt
> ½ C sour cream

½ cucumber, peeled, shredded, no seeds (just peel it with a peeler until you get to the seeds - discard seeds) then chop fine.
¼ Vidalia onion, chopped fine
Cumin to taste
Cavender's to taste
Cracked black pepper to taste

Combine all ingredients, refrigerate for at least 2 hours before serving.

LOWER ALABAMA TOMATO GRAVY

Although lots of folks like their tomato gravy as a breakfast dish (over grits or biscuits), at our house we use this for dinner, served over rice, grits or any other "starch."

3 T bacon grease
3 T AP flour
1 ⅓ C chicken stock/broth
1 15 oz can diced tomatoes, with liquid
dash S&P

In a cast-iron skillet over medium heat, whisk the flour into the bacon grease. Stirring constantly, cook until flour is light brown. Whisk in chicken broth and stir until smooth with no lumps. Add the tomatoes and a dash of salt and pepper. Cook until thickened, stirring constantly, about 6 minutes.

CHAPTER 12

STEWS, SOUPS & SANDWICHES

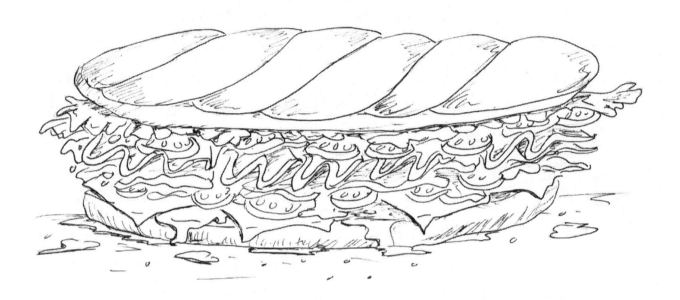

THAI SOUP (aka Tom Kha or Tom Kha Gai)
The "Gai" part of the soup translates to me, roughly, "with chicken." All we can present here is a bastardized version of the Thai national soup. Eric has been making this soup for decades, when we used to have to bring our seasonings back from Thailand. Now, you should be able to find the ingredients at any Asian or specialty market, here in the South.

    1-2 T coconut oil
    ½ large yellow onion, sliced thinly
    4 cloves garlic, smashed and diced
    1 jalapeno pepper, sliced, OR 2 green chiles
    3 slices ginger, ¼ inch apiece
    1 stalk lemongrass, washed and sliced into 2-3" pieces
    2 T Thai Tom Yam paste (more to taste added before serving is ok too)
    4 C chicken broth
    4 C coconut milk (canned)
    2 C fresh chicken, deboned
    1 C mushrooms, washed and sliced
    1 zucchini quartered and sliced
    1-2 t fish sauce
    3 T lime juice
    3 green onions, thinly sliced

Cilantro, washed and chopped (optional)

Either start by placing 6 chicken thighs in a pan and cover with water, bring to boil and cook till falling apart. Remove chicken and debone, discard skin, reserve stock. Or you can use boneless/skinless chicken and use chicken stock/bouillon for a faster start.

Heat the coconut oil in a medium-sized saucepan over medium heat. Add onion, garlic, jalapeno, ginger, zucchini, lemongrass and Thom Yam paste. Cook, stirring often, until onions are soft. Add broth; bring to a boil. Lower heat and simmer, uncovered, for about a half-hour.

Add coconut milk, chicken breast (or shrimp, peeled and deveined) and mushrooms. Simmer together until chicken (or shrimp) is cooked. Shrimp only takes 3-5 minutes. Don't overcook! Add fish sauce and lime juice to taste. Adjust seasonings to your liking. Cook 2 minutes more, then ladle into bowls over rice (or with rice on the side), garnished with the green onions and cilantro. VARIATIONS: you can make a meatless version (which would be Tom Kha), which is almost as tasty.

LOWER ALABAMA-STYLE HUNGARIAN GOULASH
(From Theresa)
It was my first trip to Europe, back around 1986. We flew from Nashville International Airport and, with thunderstorms and several delays, finally landed at our initial destination, Vienna, Austria. After such a long day of traveling, we checked into our hotel, then went out in search of supper. By this time, it was 10 p.m., and not many restaurants were still serving. There was one tiny, "hole-in-the-wall" Hungarian restaurant down a dark, narrow, cobblestoned street, and they were happy to seat us. They told us, in a blend of broken English and hand gestures, that they only had one thing left that was still hot in the kitchen, and that was Goulash. Served with a hearty bread and a robust, dry red wine, this was one of the meals I still remember after all these decades. This is as close as I can approximate that dish.

1 ½ lbs stew beef, cut into 1-inch cubes
¼ - ½ C AP flour with S&P
2 t butter, unsalted
2 large Vidalia onions, chopped well
5 cloves garlic, peeled, smashed and chopped
1 t caraway seeds
4 C beef broth
1/4 C Hungarian paprika
1 ½ C tomatoes, diced (or the canned equivalent, but drained, reserve juice)
2 Bay leaves
Dash S&P
1 ½ C carrots, sliced
2 bell peppers, washed, seeded and chopped
3 C potatoes, washed and cubed

In a bag, put flour, salt and pepper and shake to blend. Add meat cubes to the bag and coat. Sear the meat in a Dutch oven with butter over medium-high heat; set meat aside.

Melt butter in Dutch oven; saute onions until translucent. Add garlic and caraway seeds and cook for about 2 minutes or until you can smell the garlic. Use a little of the broth to deglaze the pan, then return meat to the pan. Stir and add paprika; add the rest of the broth, tomatoes, Bay leaves and a dash of salt and pepper.

Bring to a low boil, then cover. Simmer on low for about 45 minutes or until meat is tender. Add carrots, peppers and potatoes and simmer for about another 30 minutes. Serve topped with a dollop of sour cream and a good, hot, hearty bread. Leftovers are exceptionally good!

JUST WEST OF PARIS FRENCH ONION SOUP
(From Theresa)
My first time in France, I headed for Paris, eager to try some true French Onion Soup. I had it on a lovely afternoon at a restaurant called "L'Escargots" (which still exists). It was instant love! Here's my version.

> 2 cans (10.5 ounces each) condensed beef broth
> 2 cans water
> ¼ C butter, unsalted
> 1-2 t. Worcestershire sauce
> 2 large yellow onions (I have had good luck with Vidalias), chopped
> 2 t brown sugar

Melt butter in Dutch oven; stir in Worcestershire sauce and sugar. Add onions. Bake in oven set at 325 degrees for about 2 ½ hours, stirring every half-hour or so, until onions look a deep golden brown. Remove to stove top. Add broth and water and heat to boiling, then simmer for 10-15 minutes. Serve in heated bowls with crusty French bread and croutons on top (see that recipe, below).

Note: you might think it's a typo about the brown sugar, but adding just this tiny amount gives the beef broth a depth of flavor that it won't have otherwise.

HOMEMADE CROUTONS
We made these using some of my leftover bread, the recipe for which is in Chapter 5 ("Mother Theresa's").

> 4 slices homemade or other artisan bread, thinly sliced (to about ¼" thickness)
> 4 T butter
> Dash garlic powder
> ½ C each mozzarella and parmesan cheeses, thinly sliced

Spread equal amounts of butter on each slice of bread; place slices on baking pan lined with parchment paper (you will have a sticky mess if you use foil). Sprinkle slices with garlic powder; cover each slice with mozzarella slices. Turn broiler on "low" and broil until mozzarella is melted but not burned. Pull out pan and add parmesan cheese; put in broiler, this time set on "high," and keep a close eye as it can burn quickly. Remove from oven when the cheese is browned to your liking.

Put slices on cutting board; cut into pieces to go into the serving bowls, as a topping for French Onion Soup.

EASY, DELECTABLE, CREAM OF ARTICHOKE SOUP
(From Theresa)
Back around 1992, we had a Christmas family reunion in Key West, Florida. One "kid-less" night, we grown-ups went out to a French restaurant. I ordered a soup, which, upon tasting, thought, "I can make this, or something like this, at home." Now, mind you, this version does not claim to be any kind of gourmet soup; but it's hearty and delicious, and makes a perfect meal when paired with a light white wine and a crusty French bread. Just don't tell anyone how easy it is! They'll think you're a culinary genius.

    1 can Cream of Mushroom soup
    2 C 2 percent milk
    1 8-oz jar marinated artichokes (with marinade)
    1 small jar pimientos, drained
    S&P if desired

Put all ingredients *except* pimientos in blender. Pulse on low until fairly smooth. Pour into a saucepan, then add drained pimientos. Cook on low until heated through (if you cook this on too high a heat, the milk will clabber. It won't affect the taste but it won't be pretty).

About the pimientos: if you whir them in the blender with everything else, it will make the soup pink—which is what you might like if you're making this for a special occasion, such as Valentine's Day!

ENGLISH CLASS PERFECT GRILLED CHEESE
(From Theresa)
In my last 17 years of teaching, I found myself teaching high school English, after many other years of Physical Education teaching elementary school students. Those last years were my most stressful, but probably my most rewarding–I actually found I could develop a rapport with these students who were, in fact, young adults. I also found that, especially for teenagers (who are always hungry), that when grades weren't a great motivator, food worked! So every 6-8 weeks I gave my students a good behavior celebration. I bought an electric griddle that could make 6 sandwiches at a time. My students, many of whom are friends with me on Facebook, asked that I add my "recipe" for a perfect grilled cheese sandwich, so this is dedicated to the students of Robertsdale High School (south Alabama), from the years 2005 to 2022.

This "recipe" makes one grilled cheese sandwich. Multiply accordingly.

2 pieces bread, your choice (I love Dave's Killer Bread)
2 slices Kraft or Velveeta (my two favorites)
2-3 T butter or mayonnaise (or both!)

Get your griddle hot on medium-high heat. Spread mayo-butter on each sandwich slice; cook on skillet until lightly browned. Add the cheese slices and put one of the slices of bread on top.

This is what makes the grilled cheese perfect: Many cooks say to take your spatula and "mash" the bread down as the sandwich cooks. Don't do it! Very lightly turn the sandwich, preferably only once, as it cooks to cheesy perfection. By handling the sandwich as little as possible, the bread will be crisp and buttery on the outside, yet soft and creamy on the inside. My students said, "Mrs. Lacey, you make the best grilled cheese sandwiches anywhere!"

CHAPTER 13

FRUIT AND VEGETABLE DISHES

AUNT T'S TOMATO PIE

I perfected this recipe in the summer of 2013, and "Uncle Boo" has asked me to make a pie every week that we have those delicious, summer vine-ripened tomatoes.

YOU WILL NEED:

    One Pie Crust (I use Pillsbury's but some people like to make their own)
    3 tomatoes, sliced thinly (I recommend heirloom tomatoes for best flavor)
    3 cups shredded mozzarella cheese (or cheddar and pepper jack)
    TO TASTE: black pepper, minced garlic, chopped fresh basil, parsley

SAUCE FOR THE TOP:

> 1 cup mayonnaise (I use ½ cup mayo mixed with ½ cup plain Greek yogurt)
> Hot sauce (I use ¼ cup Crystal)
> 1/8 C parsley or cilantro
> Bacon bits (about a cup)
> 1 small onion, diced (I use Vidalia)

Slice tomatoes and lay on paper towels, salted and peppered; turn after 15 minutes and do the same on the other side (you will probably need fresh paper towels). After this additional 15 minutes, the tomatoes will be properly drained.

While tomatoes are draining, put pie crust in an oven-proof skillet (my favorite is my cast-iron). Preheat oven to 400 degrees; bake crust for about 15 minutes (bubbles will have formed on the bottom part). Remove from oven.

Saute onion until brown and let cool, then add to the sauce ingredients.
Re-set oven to 350 degrees. Place ½ cup mozzarella in bottom of pie, with tomato slices on top; repeat layers, ending with tomatoes on top.

"Frost" the top layer evenly with the sauce; sprinkle with any remaining mozzarella. Add a little parmesan if you want it to brown up golden on top. Bake at 350 for 40 minutes or until sauce bubbles.

This makes great leftovers, and you can also make it in advance and reheat it for company. Enjoy!

BAKED TOMATO PRINCESS
This recipe works best with early heirloom tomatoes, or a big red tomato like a beefsteak, if you can't get an heirloom.

To serve two:
> 2 large heirloom tomatoes, washed

Slice the bottom 1/8" off. Slice the top right at the stalk. Cut center hard part from the top, making a "well" but not penetrating through to the bottom. In 2 ramekins or tapas pans, melt one teaspoon bacon fat in each.

Place tomatoes in ramekins, cut side up. Sprinkle with sea salt and pepper. Drizzle with homemade Italian dressing, and fill with the best blue cheese you can find (we used Maytag Bleu Cheese). Bake at 350 for 20-25 minutes. Heat plates; put tomatoes on plates.

Variations: Sprinkle with Cavender's Greek Seasoning, add fresh chopped oregano and a mix of feta and kalamata olives.

We had this with Austin's Cobia (see Fish section). The sauce from both of these was beyond excellent, so you might want to have some rice, grits or mashed potatoes with it. Made 5-27-2021.

EASY COLESLAW
(From Theresa)
This was the first dish I remember Mom letting me make when I was still quite small. Back then, you couldn't find pre-cut cabbage, much less one with carrots and purple cabbage, but today, why not use it and save some time?

> 1 bag mixed coleslaw blend (green and purple cabbage and shredded carrots)
> 1/2 C mayonnaise
> 2 T sugar or monk-fruit sweetener
> Splash lemon juice
> 1 T ACV
> Dash salt and pepper

In large bowl, mix all ingredients until homogenous. Fold in coleslaw and stir until well-blended. Best made the day before. Serve chilled.

ERIC'S "NOT SO FAST THERE" COLESLAW
So many restaurants serve coleslaw as a mere, thoughtless "side" and rarely is it a truly thoughtful addition to the meal. There are exceptions locally and coleslaw is such a highly "personal" thing in the South, Eric had to add his touch.

> 1 small head of green cabbage, heart removed, chopped
> 1 medium Vidalia onion, chopped
> ½ C Greek yogurt (plain)

2 T apple cider vinegar
1 T rice wine vinegar
2 T yellow mustard
½ a bell pepper - color of choice, chopped fine
2 T dill relish

Blend well, refrigerate for at least 2 hours.

GREEK COLESLAW

1 small green cabbage, heart removed, chopped and separated (no big hunks)
1 cup tzatziki sauce (see "SAUCES, ETC" in Chapter 11)
2 handfuls Kalamata olives, (pitted of course) chopped
big chunk of feta cheese, chopped
½ cucumber, peeled, quartered and chopped
½ purple onion, chopped
couple of dashes of Cavender's Greek Seasoning
Fresh Italian basil, chopped

Combine ingredients, refrigerate for at least 1 hour.

ASIAN COLESLAW

We have made a number of variations of this coleslaw, but this particular dish that Eric made was especially good. First made the night of March 1, 2022.

1:1 ratio of shredded lettuce and cabbage
½ can bean sprouts, drained
½ can water chestnuts, drained and chopped
2-3 chives, chopped
1-2 slices of purple onion, chopped
equal amounts Ponzu Citrus Seasoning and dressing
Annie's shiitake dressing

Toss all veggies together along with everything but dressings together. When ready to serve, toss with dressings. Serve on individual plates and sprinkle top with Chow-Mein Noodles.

ONION PIE

This recipe is a favorite of my sister-in-law, Cindy Barnett Lacey. In all my decades of enjoying her cooking, every dish she's turned out has been fabulous.

1 ½ C Ritz crackers, finely crushed
6 T unsalted butter, melted but not hot
2 C Vidalia onions, thinly sliced
3 eggs, slightly beaten
1 C whole milk
1 C sharp cheddar cheese, grated (or finely shredded)

Mix 1 ¼ C crushed crackers with 4 T butter. Press into a greased 8 x 11inch baking pan. In remaining butter, saute onions until translucent and limp. Spoon on top of cracker crumbs.

Mix eggs with milk; add a dash of salt & pepper and pour over onions. Sprinkle with the cheddar cheese and remaining cracker crumbs. Bake at 350 degrees for 30 minutes or until golden brown on top. After removing from oven, let sit for about 5 minutes before serving.

GAZPACHO WITH HEIRLOOM TOMATOES

We made this June 19, 2021. We were getting a bumper crop of cherry and heirloom tomatoes. This cold soup just gets better the longer it sits! We served it with a dollop of sour cream.

> 1 ½ C beef broth
> 2 double-hands full of cherry tomatoes
> 3 ripe heirloom tomatoes
> ¼ purple onion, diced
> 1 large cucumber, peeled, seeded and diced
> 3 large jalapenos, seeded and diced
> 1 C fresh basil, stemmed and chopped
> ½ C each fresh parsley, oregano, diced
> 4 cloves garlic, smashed and chopped
> Sour cream for garnish

In a chopper or food processor, place cherry tomatoes and heirlooms with the center pits removed and process. Over a large bowl, strain tomatoes, using a mesh colander to further remove seeds and skins. Add all the diced items and the broth. Chill for at least 2 hours, covered. Serve with cracked black pepper and sour cream.

Note: most recipes call for fresh radishes. We didn't have any and it tasted excellent without them.

BROCCOLI SALAD

(From Theresa)
This is my Aunt JoAnn Bagwell's recipe.

> 2 heads fresh broccoli, washed, drained and cut into florets
> ½ C chopped sweet onion (I recommend Vidalia)
> ½ C walnuts or pecans, chopped
> 1 C golden raisins (or dark if you prefer)
> ½ C celery, diced

DRESSING

> 1 C mayonnaise
> ½ C sugar, mango fruit sweetener or Splenda
> ¼ C ACV

Once you have chopped the broccoli, store it in fridge at least 2 hours or overnight. Combine dressing ingredients and store in fridge as well. In a separate container, combine onion, nuts, raisins and celery and chill for as long as you do everything else.

When ready to make the salad, place florets in serving bowl along with onions, etc., and pour dressing over them. Mix well.

GRAPE SALAD
(From Theresa)
This recipe has been a staple at every family gathering of my people since I can remember.

> 4 lbs. seedless grapes, washed, dried and halved
> 8 oz. sour cream, softened
> ½ C sugar or monk-fruit sweetener
> ½ t. each vanilla and cinnamon
> ½ C walnuts or pecans, chopped
> Dash brown sugar

Place grapes in serving dish, then mix all other ingredients. Pour the mixture over grapes; gently toss until well-blended. Sprinkle brown sugar with nuts over top. Chill until ready to serve.

SEOUL FOOD
Eric created this dish within a few days of our friend Willie Peck's unexpected death (2-14-2021). He loved exotic foods, was a fellow teacher of mine and a devoted father and husband. We dedicate this recipe to Willie.

> 3 lg cloves garlic, peeled & chopped
> 2 baby bok choy, chopped, bases discarded
> 2 T rice wine vinegar
> 1 T each soy sauce, sesame oil, and vegetable cooking oil
> 2 spring onions, chopped

Combine the oils, sauces, and other liquids in a wok. Brown garlic until it's crispy; remove with strainer and set aside. Saute the bok choy and green onions until bok choy is almost tender; add soy sauce and rice wine vinegar. Stir-fry until tender. Turn off and scatter fried garlic on top as a garnish.

AUNT JOYE BERNICE'S SEVEN-LAYER SALAD
(From Theresa)
My Aunt Joye Bernice Collins shared this recipe with me. It's a dish she made every year for just about any gathering, whether it was dinner on the grounds, a holiday get-together, a baby shower or a funeral. For those who don't like peas, you can omit them–this salad is just as good, either way.

6 C lettuce, washed and chopped
6 hard-boiled eggs, sliced
1 10-oz pkg frozen English peas, thawed
½ C green onions, washed and chopped
2 C cheese, shredded, your preference
1 C mayonnaise
dash each salt, pepper, paprika, sugar

In a large serving bowl, put half the lettuce. Begin placing other ingredients in layers, ending with the other half of the lettuce. "Frost" the top with mayonnaise, then sprinkle with salt, pepper, paprika and sugar. Best served the next day, or at least 6-8 hours. When serving time, toss all layers together, and be prepared for the raves!

ERIC'S SUPER-DELICIOUS ITALIAN-STYLE TWICE-BAKED SWEET POTATOES
First baked March 4, 2016, after I came home tired decorating for Robertsdale High School's Prom and Eric cooked and served this with steak. A sweet night.

YOU WILL NEED (for just two servings, increase accordingly for more)
One sweet potato, completely baked and peeled
1/3 block Feta cheese, crumbled
Roasted red bell pepper, cooled and minced
3 garlic cloves, minced and sautéed in butter (or mixed with olive oil)
1/3 sweet onion, diced and sautéed (I cook it with the garlic)
2 T. Oregano
4 T. Parmesan cheese

In a medium-sized glass bowl, whip the sweet potato until uniform in texture and creamy. Mix everything together EXCEPT the Parmesan cheese. When well blended, put half the mixture into two small, oven-proof bowls or ramekins sprayed with non-stick spray.

Top the mixture with the Parmesan and bake in the oven on 425 until bubbling (check it every five minutes).

When bubbling, turn the oven up to High Broil and broil for a few minutes. This will give the cheese a nice, crispy taste, while below the cheesy crust it will be creamy, savory and delicious.

SAVORY POTATOES
Eric made these 6-22-21. They were fantastic! No ketchup needed.

1 dozen potatoes (Baldwin County Creamers are our fave), washed and quartered
2 garlic cloves, smashed and minced
4-5 sprigs oregano
1 sprig sage
2-3 sprigs rosemary

Olive oil, S&P
Bacon fat, 1 T.

Wash and slice potatoes in quarters. Put bacon fat in the bottom of a cast iron skillet. Toss potatoes with everything to coat. Bake 350 for about 45 minutes, stirring every 15 minutes. Goes great with the Savory Chicken in the chapter on meats.

SOUTHERN STYLE APPLESAUCE PANCAKES
(From Theresa)
I perfected this several years ago, and it was published in *Mobile Bay* magazine December 2021.

I use unsweetened applesauce and monk fruit sweetener, which is naturally made without calories or carbohydrates. This helps make the dish more nutritious for diabetics. I also used this recipe when making quick, hand-held dishes for our first responders in the wake of Hurricane Sally, September 2020. Lacking electricity, we grilled these on our outdoor kitchen (porch) gas stove, so even the cooking method was an experiment!

    2 C self-rising flour
    1 C unsweetened applesauce
    1/2 C organic two percent milk
    1 C monk fruit sweetener
    1 t. each pumpkin pie spice and vanilla extract
    2 large eggs, beaten

Set oven to warm (170 degrees). In large mixing bowl, combine all ingredients until well-blended.

Spray skillet or electric griddle with non-stick. Over medium heat, bring skillet/griddle to 375 degrees.

Using a small serving spoon, ladle about 1/4 cup batter into skillet or griddle. Let cook until pancake edges are brown and centers are bubbly. Gently flip with a spatula and cook other side.

Place pancakes on rack centered on a cookie sheet. Place cooked pancakes on rack and in warm oven as you cook the rest. Serve warm with your favorite syrups, fruit or other toppings.

Serves about 6.

SAVORY POTATO PANCAKES
(From Theresa)
This is a perfect way to use leftover mashed potatoes. Some of my keto-loving friends have had good success with substituting mashed cauliflower for the potatoes.

4 C mashed potatoes
2 large eggs, beaten
1/4 C each self-rising flour and cornmeal
Dash salt, pepper and garlic powder
4 T chives, finely snipped
Dash each of oregano, basil, parsley, marjoram and thyme
1/2 C Gouda cheese, shredded
Butter and olive oil for cooking

Mix all except fats together in a medium bowl until well blended. In a heavy skillet on medium to medium-high heat (don't let it smoke!), let butter melt and mix with oil. When hot, use a large tablespoon or a serving spoon to place dollops of batter in the skillet. Gently turn when edges of potato pancakes are brown. Try to turn only once.

Serve warm with ketchup and sour cream. Serves 5-6.

EGGPLANT PARMESAN
This baked dish is lower in calories, but the way Eric cooked it, you won't know it's lower in fat than the usual, classic (fried) dish. We had this the night of June 28, 2021. I wished I had had extra room in my stomach, so I could eat more!

1 large eggplant, washed, peeled, and sliced into ¼" pieces
Sea salt
Two eggs, beaten
3 cloves garlic, smashed and minced
¼ Vidalia onion, finely chopped
1 jalapeno pepper, finely chopped
Handful fresh oregano, basil, chopped
½ lb shredded Italian blend cheese
¼ C powdered Parmesan cheese (Kraft)
¼ C Italian seasoning
¾ C plain breadcrumbs
1 t. olive oil
1 jar Alessi marinara (chunky)
¼ C white wine
¼ stick butter, melted
½ pkg Dreamfield noodles
6 c water, boiling

Lay eggplant slices on paper towels. Dust one side with salt. Wait 15 minutes, flip, and do the other side. Meanwhile, take garlic, onion, and jalapeno; saute in half the butter. Add marinara sauce, rinse the jar with the white wine, pour resulting liquid into the pot. Let it bubble 20-30 minutes, stirring frequently.

Wipe off eggplant with paper towels. Dredge in egg wash and roll in the mixed, dry ingredients. Put on a cookie sheet (with a baking rack) coated with nonstick spray; bake at 350 approx. 10 minutes per side, until eggplant has developed a brown and crusty surface.

Put about half of the marinara sauce in an 8 x 12 casserole pan sprayed with nonstick. Put the eggplant in layers, covered with chopped Italian-blend cheese. Put remaining marinara on top. Layer it with the rest of the cheese. Add ½ bag shredded Parmesan cheese and the fresh herbs. Bake at 350 for about 30 minutes until bubbling. Top with leftover breadcrumbs and herbs and broil until top is crunchy and brown.

Remove from oven, let rest about 10-15 minutes. While eggplant is resting put noodles in pan and boil until al dente. Drain noodles. Put eggplant on top of noodles. Best served with crusty French bread and on warm plates.

POTATOES FLORENTINE
Eric created this in August of 2021. It became an instant classic and could make a meal in itself! This particular dish serves two people.

    1 large baking potato, washed, peeled and sliced into ½" flats
    Water to cover
    Dash sea salt
    Couple sprigs rosemary, whole
    Oregano, basil, white mushrooms, washed and sliced
    Vidalia onion, chopped
    Prosciutto, chopped
    1 C Swiss cheese
    1 pkg. frozen chopped spinach, thawed and drained well
    3 T. heavy cream
    ¼ C parmesan cheese, grated
    2 cloves garlic, peeled and chopped
    Butter (enough to saute veggies and herbs)
    1 t. olive oil

In a heavy skillet, cover potato slices with water and rosemary and boil about 10 minutes. Carefully remove potato slices from water and empty pan. In butter and olive oil, brown potatoes on both sides in skillet. Put in oven at 275.

Prepare the rest of the ingredients while potatoes are baking. In a cast iron skillet, chopped 1 ½ cups of prosciutto and saute for 6-10 minutes. Add to this melted butter and add garlic, chopped veggies and mushrooms until soft. Add spinach and stir. Add cream and keep stirring. Add the grated Swiss cheese and herbs. Remove from heat. Take this mixture and cover potatoes with it. Sprinkle parmesan cheese on top. Bake at 350 for about 30 minutes.

CREAMY MASHED POTATOES
(From Theresa)
This is one of the first "hot" dishes my mom would let me make. Leftovers make really good mashed potato pancakes. That recipe is a few pages before this one.

> 4 large potatoes (I like Yukon Gold), washed and sliced to ¼" thickness
> Water to cover potatoes
> 2 T Italian seasoning
> 1 T each salt and pepper
> ½ C to 1 C milk
> ½ block cream cheese, cubed
> Parsley or paprika to garnish (your choice—or both)

Prepare potatoes and bring water to a low boil. Add Italian seasoning and S&P to water, then carefully add potatoes so as not to burn yourself. Boil, covered, until tender, about 20 or so minutes (altitude will affect cook time). Test with a fork for tenderness.
 When tender to your liking, carefully drain potatoes using a colander, and return to pan. With flame on low, add milk, ¼ C at a time, and cream cheese, a few cubes at a time. Stir or whip as you go, being careful not to make the potatoes too "soupy." Fold into serving bowl and garnish. Serve immediately.

CREAMY MASHED TURNIPS

> 4-5 ripe turnips, washed, peeled and cubed (cross-cut if needed to get in water)
> water (enough to cover turnips)
> 2 T chicken bouillon
> 2-4 T butter
> ⅓ C Cream cheese, softened
> ½ C sour cream
> dash each garlic powder & Cachere's

Boil turnips in water with chicken bouillon until turnips are soft. Drain. In mixing bowl, add all other ingredients. Adjust to how creamy you like the turnips, mashing turnips into ingredients. Taste occasionally. This recipe will serve 3-4.

ERIC'S CABBAGE AND PEANUT STIR-FRY
Eric cooked this the night of November 14, 2019. It was just the two of us, thus, a good night to experiment. It was fantastic! Note: this recipe is also in the seafood chapter, but we omitted the shrimp and fish, here.

Chop the following:
> ½ cabbage head, then quartered, then slice vertically so it's chopped
> 1 cup salted peanuts, chopped
> ¼ Vidalia onion, finely cut

In a small bowl, combine 1 cup creamy or whipped peanut butter, 2 T Rice Wine Vinegar, 1 tsp minced garlic, 2 T soy sauce and juice of half a lime. Toss mixture together and add a big dash of pepper. Let sit for a while.

In a wok, heat a little olive oil and butter until hot but not smoking. Add cabbage and onion, stirring constantly, until cooked but not soft. Toss in peanut butter-soy sauce mixture and peanuts and stir. Cook until heated through. You can enjoy this "as is," or add a protein—even tofu.

GREEK SALAD
  This is a favorite of ours. You can add cooked seafood, chicken, pork or beef, or just as a meatless dinner. Unlike many salads, this one is also good the next day.

> 1 block Feta cheese, chopped
> 1 C Green olives, chopped and pitted
> 1 C Kalamata olives, same
> 12 Cherry tomatoes, halved
> 1 Bell pepper, finely chopped (can be yellow, red or green)
> Half a cucumber, peeled and chopped, or sliced if you prefer
> Cavender's Greek seasoning to taste
> Olive oil
> Balsamic vinegar
> *Tzatziki sauce adds a great creamy substrate to this when adding to pasta (See "SAUCES, etc." in Chapter 11).

Make a Greek salad with the veggies and feta and put it in a bowl. Add olive oil, Greek seasoning and balsamic and mix well (but gently).

SOUTHERN FRIED SWEET CORN (RIFF)
We first created this May 14, 2020. You can get Silver Queen corn from Florida as early as mid-May, and we found it at a local produce shop (Allegri's). It was refrigerated from the moment of harvest until I shucked it in the backyard. After dinner we sat out on the porch, enjoying the evening until a swarm of newly-hatched mosquitoes invaded and chased us indoors.

> 4 ears fresh Silver Queen corn
> ½ medium Vidalia onion, chopped
> ¼ green bell pepper, chopped
> 1 stick unsalted butter
> 1 T. cream cheese, whipped
> Cracked black pepper
> ½ C Half & Half
> Chachere's to taste (after cooking)

Shuck the corn and slice off the cob. Saute the onion and bell pepper in half the butter. After the onion is translucent and pepper is soft; add the corn to the skillet and continue sautéing for about 15 minutes, stirring frequently.

Add a quarter of the stick of butter and stir for 5-10 minutes until absorbed. Add Half and Half and continue to saute until absorbed. Add a T. of the whipped cream cheese and stir until absorbed. Turn off the heat, let sit for 15 minutes while you have a Boodles gin & tonic and sit on the back porch, reminisce and look to the future.

Add the remaining butter and stir everything together until bubbling. Serve immediately with the Chachere's.

This particular recipe usually serves 4, or if you have many other dishes, break the cobs in half so it serves 8.

DEBBIE LITTLE'S BROCCOLI SALAD

Debbie is one of the co-owners of Dry Ridge Outfitters in Driggs, Idaho. Back in the summer of 2002, we went horse-camping for a week in the Teton Mountain Range, led by her husband (Kevin) and son. An amazing trip—we had a snow-ball fight on a glacier and woke up one morning to see a mother MOOSE giving her baby a bath in a neighboring pond! Anyway, Debbie made this in advance for us to enjoy while "on the trail."

3 bunches broccoli
Small red onion (optional)
Shredded cheddar cheese
½ C mayo
½ C apple cider vinegar
1/3 C sugar, monk-fruit sweetener or honey
1 pound bacon, cooked and crumbled

Cook bacon until crisp to your liking. Chop broccoli in bite-size pieces; chop onion; shred cheese. Mix together, then add the sugar/vinegar mixture and add mayo to taste.

INDEX (CROSS-REFERENCED)   PAGE(S)